Student Interactive

myView®
LITERACY
4

SAVVAS
LEARNING COMPANY

Cover: Fer Gregory/Shutterstock; TJ Brown/Shutterstock; Nathapol Kongseang/Shutterstock; Surachai/Shutterstock; Jim Parkin/123RF; Eric Isselee/Shutterstock; Dave Watts/Alamy; Thawat Tanhai/123RF GB Ltd; Iakov Filimonov/Shutterstock; Aslysun/Shutterstock; Art Collection 3/Alamy Stock Photo; Igor Kyrlytsya/Shutterstock; Robert_S/Shutterstock; Africa Rising/Shutterstock; LouieLea/Shutterstock; Jixin Yu/Shutterstock; Pingvin_house/Shutterstock

Attributions of third party content appear on page 432, which constitutes an extension of this copyright page.

ISBN-13: 978-0-134-90884-7
ISBN-10: 0-134-90884-8

12 22

Julie Coiro, Ph.D.

Jim Cummins, Ph.D.

Pat Cunningham, Ph.D.

Elfrieda Hiebert, Ph.D.

Pamela Mason, Ed.D.

Ernest Morrell, Ph.D.

P. David Pearson, Ph.D.

Frank Serafini, Ph.D.

Alfred Tatum, Ph.D.

Sharon Vaughn, Ph.D.

Judy Wallis, Ed.D.

Lee Wright, Ed.D.

UNIT 1

Networks

Adaptations

Networks

Essential Question

How can a place affect how we live?

 Watch

"Getting to School"

TURN and TALK

How do you travel to different places in your community?

SAVVAS
realize⸱⸱⸱
Go ONLINE for
all lessons.

- ▶ VIDEO
- 🔊 AUDIO
- 👆 INTERACTIVITY
- 🎮 GAME
- ✏️ ANNOTATE
- 📖 BOOK
- 🔍 RESEARCH

READING WORKSHOP

READING-WRITING BRIDGE

- Academic Vocabulary • Word Study
- **Read Like a Writer** • **Write for a Reader**
- Spelling • Language and Conventions

WRITING WORKSHOP

- Introduce and Immerse • Develop Elements   **Personal Narrative**
- Develop Structure • Writer's Craft
- Publish, Celebrate, and Assess

PROJECT-BASED INQUIRY

- Inquire • Research • Collaborate

UNIT
1

Independent Reading

You can become a lifelong reader by reading often and by exploring many kinds of texts. In this unit, you will read assigned texts with your teacher. You will also choose other texts to read during independent reading.

Follow these steps to help you select a book you will enjoy reading on your own.

Step 1 Make a plan for choosing a book at the right level. Ask yourself:

- What titles have I enjoyed reading in the past?

- How can I choose a book that is interesting and challenging and that I can understand independently?

Step 2 Select a book and open it to any two pages. Use this strategy to determine if the book is just right for you.

Is this book right for me?
Read the two pages you turned to and then ask yourself:

	YES	NO
Do I understand most of the words?	○	○
Are there one or two words that I have to sound out?	○	○
Are there interesting features, such as pictures and headings?	○	○

Independent Reading Log

Date	Book	Genre	Pages Read	Minutes Read	My Ratings
					☆☆☆☆☆

Unit Goals

Shade in the circle to rate how well you meet each goal now.

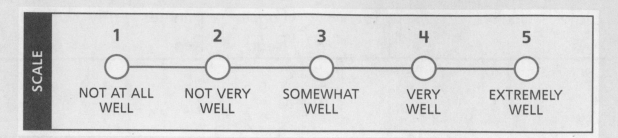

SCALE	1	2	3	4	5
	○	○	○	○	○
	NOT AT ALL WELL	NOT VERY WELL	SOMEWHAT WELL	VERY WELL	EXTREMELY WELL

Reading Workshop

	1	2	3	4	5
I know about different types of narrative nonfiction and understand their elements.	○	○	○	○	○

Reading-Writing Bridge

	1	2	3	4	5
I can use language to make connections between reading narrative nonfiction and writing a personal narrative.	○	○	○	○	○

Writing Workshop

	1	2	3	4	5
I can use elements of narrative nonfiction writing to write a personal narrative.	○	○	○	○	○

Unit Theme

	1	2	3	4	5
I can determine how a place can affect how we live.	○	○	○	○	○

Academic Vocabulary

Use these vocabulary words to talk and write about this unit's theme, *Networks: contribute, exposed, habit, severe,* and *significant*.

TURN and TALK Read the vocabulary words and related words in the chart. With a partner, use each newly acquired vocabulary word in a sentence to show its relationship to another word or concept. For example, *give* and *contribute* are related because *giving* is one way to *contribute*. *The baseball club needed money for equipment, so they asked me to* **contribute**.

Academic Vocabulary	Related Words	Used in a Sentence
contribute	donate, assist	
exposed	revealed, unprotected	
habit	usual, practice	
severe	harsh, serious	
significant	important, relevant	

INTERACTIVITY

DISCOVER
Extraordinary Iceland

PEOPLE LIVE HERE! Iceland is very far north. In summer, daylight lasts roughly twenty hours. In winter, there can be fewer than four hours of daylight. How would this affect you if you lived here?

SUMMER
20 HRS.

WINTER
4 HRS.

REYKJANES PENINSULA This area is home to what local people refer to as lava fields. These form after a volcanic eruption when a lava flow cools and hardens. There are also mud pools here.

Scalding-hot mud bubbles up through cracks in the earth.

ASKJA CALDERA Some volcanoes collapse after they erupt, forming a large depression called a *caldera*. Askja Caldera is very rocky and is covered in black volcanic sand. A large lake and hot springs form part of the landscape. Not much grows here, making it hard for humans and animals to live here.

Weekly Question

How can visiting new places expand our understanding of our place in the world?

TURN and TALK How is Iceland different from where you live? Engage in a one-on-one discussion with your partner. Listen carefully, and build on your partner's comments.

THE PERFECT LANDSCAPE

In 1965 and 1967, astronauts were preparing to go to the moon. Iceland was the perfect place for them to train because it also has a harsh landscape. It's a young, volcanic country. The rocks are not exceptionally old compared to other places on Earth. The astronauts visited the Askja Caldera and the Reykjanes Peninsula to learn more about what it might be like on the moon.

Learning Goal

I can learn more about narrative nonfiction by analyzing the author's purpose in an autobiography.

Spotlight on Genre

Narrative Nonfiction

Narrative nonfiction is informational text that tells a story about real people and events. It includes

- A **purpose,** or the author's reason for writing
- **Descriptive details** about real people and events
- **Chronological,** or time order, structure

Although narrative nonfiction shares these characteristics, there are many different types of narrative nonfiction. This week you will be reading an **autobiography**, which is a true story about the author's own life.

A text that tells a story, but with real people and events, is narrative nonfiction.

TURN and TALK Describe to a partner a story you have read about a real person or event. Use the anchor chart to tell how you know whether the story is narrative nonfiction. Take notes and then share your ideas with the class.

My NOTES

_____

_____

_____

_____

_____

_____

_____

NARRATIVE NONFICTION ANCHOR CHART

→ PURPOSE:

-To inform, to entertain

→ FEATURES:

-Describes a true event or series of events

-Uses literary characteristics also found in fiction, such as:

* Setting
* Figurative language
* Plot elements (rising action, climax, falling action, and resolution)

→ TYPES:

Autobiography, biography, diary or journal, memoir, interview

Buzz Aldrin is best known as an astronaut on the historic *Apollo 11* mission. He has devoted his life to the study of space. He also has great hopes for the future of space exploration. He believes that "the next monumental achievement of humanity will be the first landing by an Earthling, a human being, on the planet Mars."

Reaching for the Moon

Preview Vocabulary

As you read *Reaching for the Moon*, pay attention to these vocabulary words. Notice how they can help you understand the author's purpose.

> determination   independence
>
> specialized   struggled   confidence

Read

Use the strategies in the First Read boxes to help you set a purpose for reading. Active readers of **narrative nonfiction** follow these strategies when they read a text the first time.

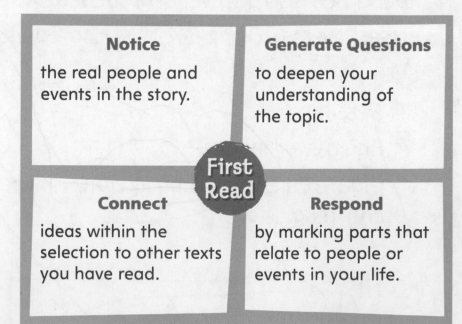

Notice the real people and events in the story.

Generate Questions to deepen your understanding of the topic.

First Read

Connect ideas within the selection to other texts you have read.

Respond by marking parts that relate to people or events in your life.

Reaching for the Moon

by Buzz Aldrin

AUDIO

ANNOTATE

Explain Author's Purpose

<u>Underline</u> one or more sentences that show why Buzz Aldrin begins his story by talking about his childhood.

1   The name my parents gave me was Edwin Eugene, but the name my sister gave me was the one that would stay with me all my life. Since I was the only son, everyone in my family called me Brother. But my sister Fay Ann, a year older than I was, could only manage to say "Buzzer." Later it got shortened to "Buzz," and no one ever called me anything else.

2   On summer nights the Moon hung low in the sky, so close to our house that I thought I could reach out and touch the soft white light. I never imagined that one day I would walk on its surface. But maybe it was meant to be. You see, before she was married, my mother's last name was Moon.

3   My father's job with Standard Oil took him all over the country, and he flew his own plane from coast to coast. During World War II he served in the Army Air Corps and came home for visits, looking tall and important in his colonel's uniform.

4   When I was two years old, my father took me flying for the first time, in a small, shiny white plane painted to look like an eagle. I was a little frightened as the plane shuddered into flight. But mostly I was thrilled. I loved the speed, the sense of soaring high above the Earth, supported only by the air passing around the metal wings.

5   One day I would fly in a different machine called the *Eagle*—but that would be many years in the future and a very different kind of adventure.

CLOSE READ

Use Text Evidence

Highlight evidence in the text that helps you determine the author's purpose.

Vocabulary in Context

Readers can determine the meanings of unfamiliar words by using context clues. Use context clues to determine the meaning of *precious*. Underline the context clues that support your definition.

6   Usually there was plenty to hold my attention right here on Earth. My family spent many summers at Culver Lake in the Appalachian Mountains, and one summer, when I was about six or seven, I began collecting rocks. There was treasure everywhere I looked. Those rocks were precious, they were beautiful, and—most importantly—they were *mine*.

7   One morning I gathered up the best of my rocks, put them in a bucket, and carried them down to the dock to show my friend. He wanted a rock. I didn't want to give it to him. He pushed me, bucket and all, off the dock.

8   I wouldn't let go of my rocks, even though the weight of them pulled me down. The light at the surface slowly drifted away. When my friend's father pulled me out, I still had my arms wrapped around the bucket.

9   I knew that if something was important to you, you had to hold on.

10   Determination, strength, independence—those were the qualities I worshipped in my favorite movie hero, the Lone Ranger. I went to the movies every Saturday, and sometimes I even snuck in through the fire escape when I didn't have the money to buy a ticket. I felt just like the Lone Ranger the day I set off to ride my bike across the George Washington Bridge to New York City. Ten years old, I pedaled twenty miles down unfamiliar roads and busy streets, past neighbors and strangers, out into the unknown. Just like the Lone Ranger, I didn't need help from anyone. It took me all day, but I found the way and did it myself.

11   Almost every day I played some kind of sport, from swimming to high school track to pick-up games of football in the park across the street. The older boys let me play because although I was small, I was tough.

CLOSE READ

Explain Author's Purpose

Authors include **anecdotes**, or brief self-contained stories, in longer texts. The purpose of the anecdote is often to strengthen the message or impact of the whole text.

Identify and underline an anecdote. Then underline details that help explain why Buzz Aldrin included the anecdote.

determination the will to achieve a difficult task

independence freedom from being controlled or needing help from others

Explain Author's Purpose

Underline details in paragraphs 13–16 that explain why Buzz Aldrin tells about working hard at West Point.

12   No matter what the sport, I played every game hard, because I wanted to win. I loved being part of a team, working together to fight for victory. But it was even better to compete on my own, like when I flew over the bar in pole-vaulting. Then it was just me trying, with everything I had, to be the best. Whether I won or lost was up to me.

13   When I finished high school, my father wanted me to go to the naval academy, but I chose West Point instead. I wasn't interested in the Navy; I wanted to be in the Air Force. And I thought West Point would help me get there.

14   That first summer at West Point was the toughest challenge I had faced. We had to run everywhere; no walking was allowed. We couldn't speak during meals. Every order from an upperclassman or a teacher had to be obeyed at once.

15   I followed every order. I studied every night. By the end of the year I was first in my class. By the end of four years I had the grades to do whatever I wanted—and what I wanted more than anything was to fly!

16   After West Point I joined the Air Force, at last, and learned to fly fighter jets, fast and quick in the sky. I loved the feeling of breaking free from gravity. I loved going as fast as a human being could go.

17   When I finished my training, I flew sixty-six combat missions in the Korean War.

18   After the war I was stationed in Germany, learning to pilot planes that flew faster than the speed of sound. But there were men flying faster than that— America's first seven astronauts, the men in the Mercury program. Their goal was to be the first Americans to orbit the earth.

19   The astronauts seemed like supermen to me. I couldn't imagine myself exploring outer space. But that changed when my friend Ed White from West Point told me his plan to apply to the space program. That was when I realized that the Mercury astronauts were pilots just like Ed—and just like me.

20   I already flew the fastest planes on Earth. But Mercury was a brand-new adventure. It was America's first step into space. And I wanted to be a part of it.

21   I was already a good pilot. But the Air Force had many good pilots. I needed to find something I could do better than anyone else, something that would make me an astronaut.

CLOSE READ

Explain Author's Purpose

Underline details that help you understand why Buzz Aldrin mentions Ed White.

CLOSE READ

Explain Author's Purpose

<u>Underline</u> details that Buzz Aldrin uses to show his determination.

specialized gained specific knowledge

22   I went back to a university, to the same school my father had gone to, and studied aeronautics and astronautics. I specialized in something called rendezvous, learning how to bring two different objects together in space.

23   Computers could do most of the work for rendezvous, but I believed that pilots needed to understand it themselves, in case something went wrong. A computer can calculate numbers faster than the human brain; but people bring creativity and common sense to a problem, something a computer cannot do.

24   I dedicated my final paper to the American astronauts: "Oh, that I were one of them."

25   The first time I applied to the astronaut program, I wasn't accepted. But I didn't give up. When I applied a second time, I got in. I tried to appear as if I'd always known I'd make it, but inside I was bursting with excitement. I was already a pilot and a scientist: now I was an astronaut as well.

26   Along with the other men in the space program, I studied computers and instruments, what went right and what went wrong on each previous spaceflight, and how to survive in the wilderness if my spacecraft crashed returning to Earth. We also had to learn to move in the weightlessness of space. The others trained with a system of ropes and pulleys, but I thought training underwater would work much better. I spent hours in the pool tethered to an air line. The simplest movements—turning a handle, tightening a screw—had to be practiced over and over again.

Explain Author's Purpose

What details in the text does the illustration help bring to life? <u>Underline</u> those details.

27 My first spaceflight was on board *Gemini 12*. My mission, along with my fellow astronaut Jim Lovell, was to orbit the Earth and to practice rendezvous techniques with another vehicle in space.

28 Once the spacecraft was in orbit, I put on my space suit, opened the hatch, and drifted out into space. Only a thin cord connected me to *Gemini* as we circled the Earth at 17,500 miles per hour, five miles every second. It took us less than two hours to go all the way around the world.

29 But the speed didn't seem real to me. I felt as if I were gently floating while the Earth spun beneath me. I could see the great curve of my home planet: the brown mass of Africa, night falling over the Indian Ocean, a shower of green meteors tumbling into the Australian desert.

30   After *Gemini 12*, there was a new mission—Apollo. The goal of Apollo was to put humans on the Moon.

31   Many people thought it couldn't be done. They thought that the powerful rockets needed to go that far could never be built. They thought that computers could never do all the calculations. They thought that, even if we did reach the Moon, we would never be able to take off again to come home. But, one by one, all the challenges were met.

32   Neil Armstrong, Mike Collins, and I were next in line for a spaceflight, so we were chosen as the team for *Apollo 11*—the flight that would land on the Moon.

CLOSE READ

Use Text Evidence

Highlight text that helps you identify and understand Buzz Aldrin's message.

Explain Author's Purpose

Underline a sentence that explains Buzz Aldrin's purpose for telling his story.

struggled made a great and difficult effort

confidence a feeling that a person can succeed or do well

33   Three years after my Gemini mission, I stood beside *Apollo 11*'s Saturn V rocket. It was sunrise on July 16, 1969. Neil and Mike were already in their places on board. For a few moments I was alone.

34   All my life I had struggled to learn, to compete, to succeed, so that I could be what I was in that one moment: an astronaut on a mission to the Moon. I felt nothing but calm confidence. I was sure we would make it there and back.

35   It was time for me to board.

36   Neil, Mike, and I lay side by side on three couches, tightly strapped in. Beneath us I heard a rumble, like a faraway train. But as we lifted off, the movement felt so gentle that if I had not been looking at the instruments, I would never have known we were on our way.

37   Outside the window of the *Apollo 11*, the Earth grew smaller and smaller. At last we were so far away that I could hold up my thumb and block the bright disk from my sight.

38   After five hours we could take off our space suits and helmets and move around the cabin. We ate chicken salad and applesauce for dinner, with shrimp cocktail, my favorite of our freeze-dried choices. Then it was time to rest. Wrapped in sleeping bags, we floated above the couches, comfortably weightless. For this time *Apollo 11* was our home, a tiny bubble of air and warmth speeding through the icy cold of space.

39   Four days after launch, and after traveling 240,000 miles, we were in orbit around the Moon. *Apollo* separated into two parts: *Columbia*, where Mike would wait in orbit, and the *Eagle*, the lander. The *Eagle* was powerful enough to take Neil and me down to the Moon's surface and back up to *Columbia*. But its walls were so thin, I could have punched a pencil through them if I had tried.

40   The computer had chosen a spot for the *Eagle* to land. But through the window we could see that it was too rocky. We couldn't rely on the computer to land the *Eagle* safely. We would have to do it ourselves.

41   Neil took control. I called out to let him know how far we were from the ground. Two hundred feet. One hundred. Forty. By the time the *Eagle* landed, we had used up almost all our fuel with only twenty seconds left to spare.

42   But we had made it. We were safely on the surface of the Moon. I grinned at Neil. There was no need to say anything. We had work to do.

CLOSE READ

Explain Author's Purpose

<u>Underline</u> facts that help you understand the dangers of the *Apollo 11* mission.

Explain Author's Purpose

In paragraphs 45–46, Buzz Aldrin describes the Moon. <u>Underline</u> sensory details that Buzz Aldrin uses to help you visualize being on the Moon.

Explain how this description contributes to the author's purpose.

43   Flight and spaceflight had always meant motion to me. But now the *Eagle* stood perfectly still.

44   Neil and I put on our space suits. Neil climbed out first and descended *Eagle*'s ladder to the Moon's surface. Everyone listening back on Earth heard Neil's first words: "That's one small step for … man, one giant leap for mankind."

45   I climbed down the ladder and joined Neil. There was no color on the Moon. A flat landscape of rocks and craters stretched in all directions. Everything was gray or white. The shadows and the sky above were as black as the blackest velvet I had ever seen. I exclaimed: "Magnificent desolation."

46   I could see Earth, our home, in the sky overhead—blue water, white clouds, and brown land. I could see the continents, and I knew that they were younger than the Moon dust in which Neil and I were now leaving our footprints.

47   I took out the American flag from the compartment where it was stored.

48   Neil and I could force the pole only a few inches into the Moon's soil. I knew that more than half a billion people back on Earth were watching on television, and I worried that the flag would sag or tip. But when we took our hands away, it stood straight. I snapped off a crisp salute, just as I was taught at West Point.

49   We moved quickly on to other tasks. I became a rock collector again, gathering samples for study back on Earth.

50   Still, I remember that brief moment perfectly, so many years later. I remember the pride I felt and how I imagined the pride of every American on Earth.

51   Neil and I set up a plaque that would remain on the surface of the Moon with the simple words:

52   HERE MEN FROM THE PLANET EARTH
FIRST SET FOOT UPON THE MOON
JULY 1969, A.D.
WE CAME IN PEACE FOR ALL MANKIND

CLOSE READ

Explain Author's Purpose

What important idea does the picture illustrate? <u>Underline</u> a sentence that shows the important idea communicated by the text and image.

Develop Vocabulary

In narrative nonfiction, authors choose words that vividly describe the events and people. These words help the reader better understand real events and real people.

My TURN Read the vocabulary words. Then use each new word to write a sentence that describes something Buzz Aldrin felt or experienced.

Word	Description of an Event or Feeling
determination	
independence	
specialized	
struggled	
confidence	

Check for Understanding

My TURN Look back at the text to answer the questions.

1. What characteristics and structures in the text show you that this is an autobiography? Name three.

2. What evidence from the text supports Buzz Aldrin's idea that he was meant to walk on the Moon?

3. In the text, Buzz Aldrin says that he admired the Lone Ranger. Compare Buzz Aldrin and the Lone Ranger. What qualities do they have in common?

4. Use text evidence to analyze the importance of the *Apollo 11* mission.

Explain Author's Purpose

An **author's purpose**, or reason for writing, may be to inform, entertain, persuade, or express ideas and feelings. Authors often have more than one purpose for writing. The author's purpose determines the message that the author includes in a text.

1. **My TURN** Go to the Close Read notes in *Reaching for the Moon*. Underline the parts that help you explain the author's main purpose and message in writing.

2. **Text Evidence** Use the parts you underlined to complete the chart and explain the author's purpose.

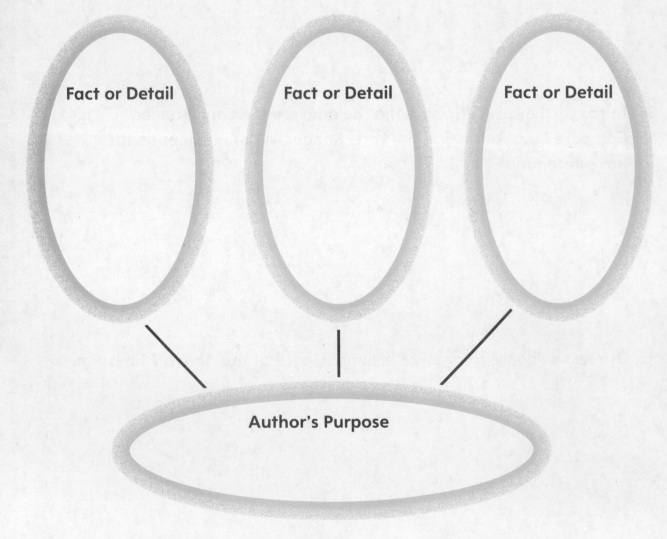

Fact or Detail

Fact or Detail

Fact or Detail

Author's Purpose

Use Text Evidence

After identifying the author's purpose, you can **use text evidence** to determine the author's message, or idea about a topic. Text evidence can be facts, details, or other information that the author includes in the text.

1. **My TURN** Go back to the Close Read notes and highlight evidence that relates to the author's purpose and message.

2. **Text Evidence** Connect your highlighted text to the author's purpose. Then use this information to explain the author's message.

Highlighted Text Evidence

Connection to Author's Purpose

Connection to Author's Message

Reflect and Share

Talk About It Buzz Aldrin described what it was like to visit space and walk on the moon. Consider all the texts you have read this week. What other new places have you read about? Use these questions to help you express an opinion about why it is important to learn about new places.

Express an Opinion When giving an opinion, express your ideas clearly and support those ideas with accurate information.

- Support your opinion with related facts and details from your reading or your own observations.
- Paraphrase information you have learned from watching videos and looking at images.
- Speak at a natural rate and volume.

Use these sentence frames to guide your responses:

I think it is important to learn about new places because . . .

What I read about _____ in _____ supports my opinion about new places.

Weekly Question

How can visiting new places expand our understanding of our place in the world?

Academic Vocabulary

Related words are words that share roots or word parts. These words can have different meanings based on how the word is used, such as *explore*, *explorer*, and *exploration*. You can learn new words from related words.

My TURN For each sentence,

1. **Use** print or digital resources, such as a dictionary or thesaurus, to find related words.

2. **Add** an additional related word in the box.

3. **Choose** the correct form of the word to complete the sentence.

Word	Related Words	Correct Form of the Word
contribute	contributes contributed _____	She _____ money to her favorite charity this year.
exposed	expose exposition _____	An explanation in writing is called an _____.
habit	habits inhabit _____	One positive _____ is exercising regularly.
severe	severely severity _____	The _____ of the storm was so great that people were encouraged to stay home.

<hr />

Learning Goal

I can use language to make connections between reading and writing.

Suffixes -ed, -ing, -s, -er, -est

The **suffixes -ed, -ing,** and **-s** can be added to verbs to tell when an action happens.

- ☾ Adding -ed to a verb means the action happened in the past.
- ☾ Adding -ing shows that the action is happening now. A verb with an -ing ending has a form of the verb to be in front of it.
- ☾ Adding -s to a verb means that the action is happening in the present.

The **suffixes -er and -est** can be added to adjectives to compare.

- ☾ Use the -er ending to compare two people or things: Her cat is younger than his dog.
- ☾ Use the -est ending to compare three or more people or things: He is the fastest runner in school.

My TURN Add -ed, -ing, and -s to each word to show when the action occurs.

Verb	Happened in the Past	Happening in the Present
orbit	orbited	is orbiting; orbits
succeed		
remember		

Read each sentence. Add -er or -est to each word in parentheses.

1. James is the _____ (fast) runner in his class.

2. Raja is _____ (tall) than his sister.

3. Keiko's voice is _____ (loud) than her best friend's.

Read Like a Writer

Authors often use graphic features, such as illustrations or photographs, to show events or portray an important idea. Through illustrations, authors help readers better understand key points in their work.

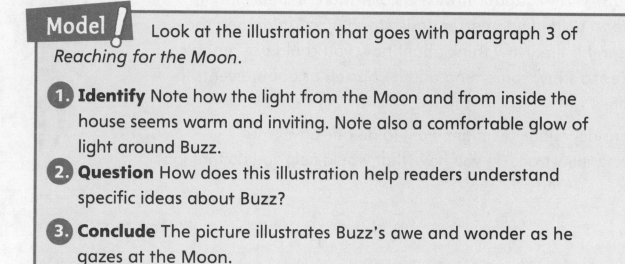

Model Look at the illustration that goes with paragraph 3 of *Reaching for the Moon*.

1. Identify Note how the light from the Moon and from inside the house seems warm and inviting. Note also a comfortable glow of light around Buzz.

2. Question How does this illustration help readers understand specific ideas about Buzz?

3. Conclude The picture illustrates Buzz's awe and wonder as he gazes at the Moon.

My TURN Look at the illustration that goes with paragraph 8 of *Reaching for the Moon*. Follow the steps to analyze it.

1. Identify The illustration shows _____

_____

2. Question How does this illustration help me understand Buzz?

3. Conclude The picture shows that Buzz_____

_____

_____

He believes that _____

_____

Write for a Reader

Pay attention to how authors use specific print and graphic features, such as text and illustrations. They help explain or emphasize important ideas and events.

Use images and illustrations to support important ideas in your writing.

My TURN Think about how the illustrations in *Reaching for the Moon* helped you better understand Buzz Aldrin and the events in his life. Now think about how you could use graphic features to show something about yourself or about events in your life.

1. Consider a job you might want to do one day. What personality traits do you have that would help you do that job?

_____

_____

2. Draw a picture that shows the job you described or that shows an event from your life that relates to that job. Add a caption or labels to the picture to give more information.

_____

_____

Spell Words with Suffixes

Suffixes -ed, -ing, -s, -er, -est Some base words change their spelling when you add the endings -ed, -ing, -s, -er, or -est. For words that end in y, drop the y and add i before adding an ending. For words ending in a consonant-vowel-consonant pattern, double the last consonant before adding an ending. For words ending in e, drop the e before adding an ending.

My TURN Sort and spell each word under the correct suffix.

SPELLING WORDS

crying	cried	cries	shipped
shipping	tagged	scarier	scariest
sadder	saddest	earlier	earliest
lazier	laziest	supplies	denied
tying	prettier	prettiest	huger

-ed

-ing

-s

-er

-est

Subjects and Predicates

A sentence has two parts: the **subject** and the **predicate**. The **subject** tells who or what the sentence is about. The **predicate** describes the subject's action or state of being. A **complete subject** contains a subject and other words including modifiers. A **complete predicate** contains an action or state of being verb and other words including modifiers.

My TURN Identify the complete subject and the complete predicate in these sentences. Underline the complete subject once and the complete predicate twice.

1. Buzz Aldrin's father served in the Army Air Corps.

2. Edwin Eugene Aldrin has a famous nickname.

3. The American flag stands on the moon today.

My TURN Edit this draft by adding complete subjects and predicates to clarify the meaning of the paragraph.

> Buzz Aldrin and Neil Armstrong were. They landed on the moon in the *Eagle*. Had to land the *Eagle* themselves. The computer had chosen a spot that was too rocky. When they finally made it to the surface. Then they got to work!

Personal Narrative

A **personal narrative** is a true story about a real experience in the writer's life. Like many fictional stories, a personal narrative is about people. It has a setting and a well-developed sequence of events. Unlike fictional stories, a personal narrative is about real people and events, and it includes the writer's thoughts and feelings about the experience.

My TURN Use a book you have read to answer the questions.

> **Learning Goal**
>
> I can use elements of narrative nonfiction writing to write a personal narrative.

The **narrator** is telling the story. Who is the **narrator**? Who are the other significant people or animals in the story?

The **setting** is the time and the place. Where and when does the narrator's experience take place?

The **sequence of events** is what happens. List three to five major events in order.

Know the Narrator

A narrative is told from the perspective of the **narrator**. Authors develop the narrator's **voice** through word choice and by deciding what information to include and what information to leave out of the text.

My TURN Choose a book you have read. Then fill in the boxes.

> How does the narrator sound? Describe the **narrator's voice** the way you would describe how a friend talks.

> Use **text evidence** to support your description of the narrator's voice.

Ask yourself why the narrator chose to tell about *this* particular experience.

Know the Setting and Events

The **sequence of events** in a personal narrative is made up of real experiences. Writers build the narrative around a problem or a conflict that exists in a particular **setting.** The sequence of events includes a beginning, a turning point, and an end. The **turning point** happens when a decision or an action brings about a change.

My TURN Work with a partner. Use a text from your classroom library to identify elements of a personal narrative.

Setting

Beginning	Turning Point	End

Brainstorm and Set a Purpose

Before writing, authors gather ideas, or **brainstorm**.

Your personal narrative will have a topic, a purpose, and an audience. The **topic** is the experience you write about. To determine your **purpose**, think about why you are writing your narrative. Do you want to entertain readers, explain something to them, or have them agree with you? To decide on your purpose, think about your readers, or your **audience**.

Describe your audience to yourself. Then decide how you want the audience to react to your personal narrative. That will help you state your purpose.

My TURN List in each column at least three experiences you have had.

Surprising Experiences	Experiences That Taught You a Lesson	Unforgettable Experiences

What is your purpose? _____

Who is your audience? _____

Which experience will be your topic? Highlight it.

Choose a meaningful experience to write about.

Plan Your Personal Narrative

Telling your story out loud can help you plan the beginning, turning point, and end of your personal narrative. It can also help you identify larger themes, or important lessons, to focus on in your writing.

My TURN Based on your topic, fill in the circles.

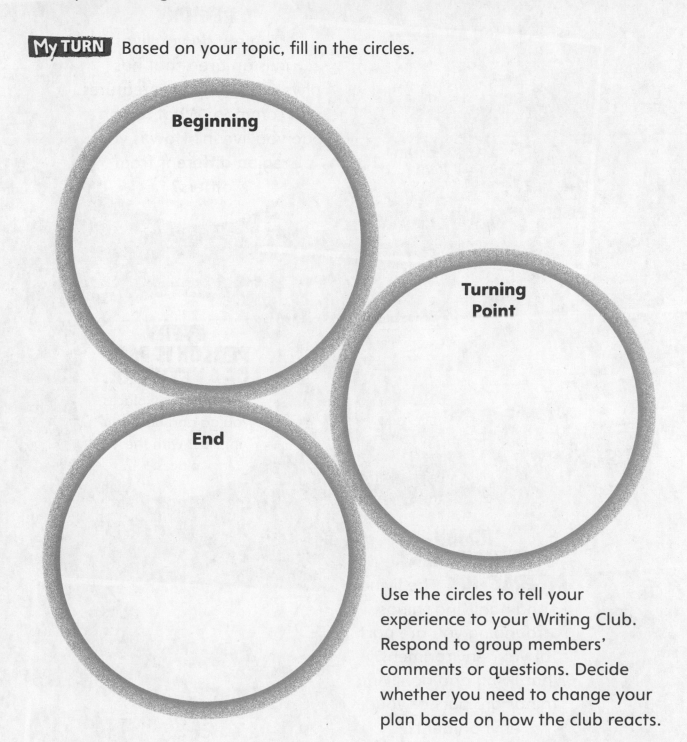

Beginning

Turning Point

End

Use the circles to tell your experience to your Writing Club. Respond to group members' comments or questions. Decide whether you need to change your plan based on how the club reacts.

INTERACTIVITY

WHERE
We Live

REGION
The region you live in is an area that has physical and human features in common. What region do you live in? How is your region different from others?

EVERY PERSON IS PART OF A NETWORK.
It includes the places you go and how you interact with these places.

HUMAN-ENVIRONMENT INTERACTION
The living and nonliving things surrounding you are part of your environment. What living and nonliving things are part of your environment?

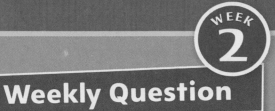

Weekly Question

In what ways can a place enrich our lives?

Quick Write Think of an important place in your network. How does the place have a personal connection to your life?

HUMAN-COMMUNITY INTERACTION

A community is a group of people who live in the same area. What places and people are in your community?

I can learn more about narrative nonfiction by analyzing how an author supports ideas with details in a biography.

Spotlight on Genre

Biography

Narrative nonfiction is informational text that tells a story about real people and events. Two types of narrative nonfiction are autobiography and biography. An **autobiography** is a true story about the author's own life. A **biography** is a true story that the author tells about another person's life.

Biographies can inform and entertain by telling interesting details about important people.

In a biography, you read a true story about a real person's life.

TURN and TALK With a partner, describe a text you have read about a historical or important person. Use the anchor chart to tell how you know if the text you read is a biography. Take notes on your discussion.

My NOTES _____

_____

_____

_____

_____

_____

BioGRaPHY
anchor CHART

PURPOSE: TO INFORM, TO ENTERTAIN,

A BioGRaPHY is:

★ written in **third-Person Point of view.**

★ organized in **chronological,** or time, **order.**

★ filled with **important facts** and **details** about the person's life.

★ written in **DESCRIPTIVE LANGUAGE** that helps the reader imagine what the person's life was really like and **WHY THE PERSON IS SPECIAL OR IMPORTANT.**

Don Brown has always been a history buff as well as a talented illustrator. As his two daughters grew older, he struggled to find inspiring books about great women in history. That prompted him to combine his love for history and his illustration skills to create the books himself!

Rare Treasure

Preview Vocabulary

As you read *Rare Treasure*, pay attention to these vocabulary words. Notice how they communicate important details in the text.

> poverty   pursued
>
> treacherous   remarkable   assembled

Read

Before you begin, establish a purpose for reading. Active readers of **narrative nonfiction** follow these strategies when they read a text the first time.

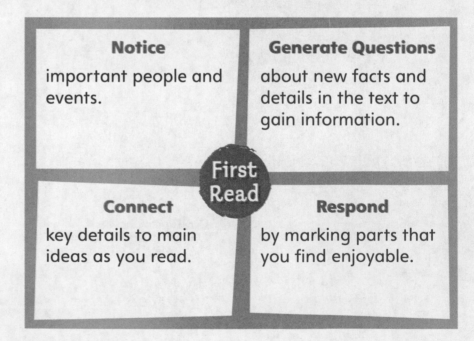

Notice
important people and events.

Generate Questions
about new facts and details in the text to gain information.

First Read

Connect
key details to main ideas as you read.

Respond
by marking parts that you find enjoyable.

Rare Treasure

MARY ANNING AND HER REMARKABLE DISCOVERIES

BY DON BROWN

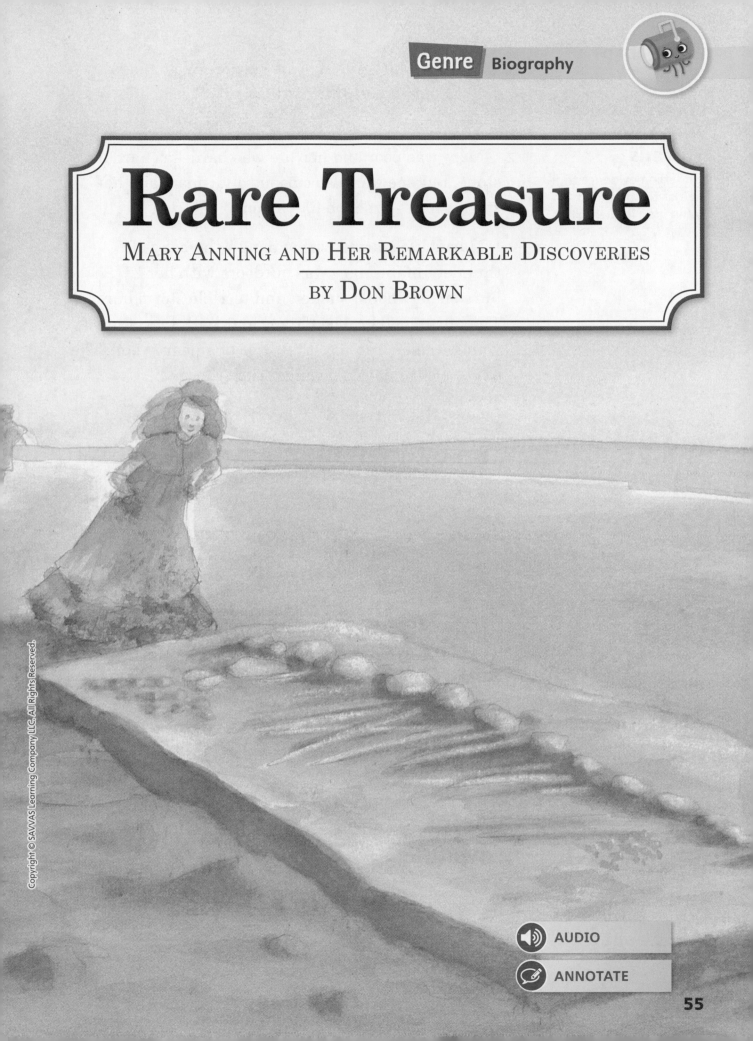

AUDIO

ANNOTATE

Analyze Main Idea and Details

Underline evidence that helps you identify a main idea in the text.

1   In 1799, Mary Anning was born in Lyme Regis, a small English port tucked tightly between cliffs and coast.

2   Mary was poor and her life was hard—as hard as stone. But she was also curious and smart and her spirit shone—it shone like a gem.

3   Mary's life started with a bang—the bang of thunder. Infant Mary was outdoors with her nursemaid when a sudden and terrible storm burst. The nursemaid grabbed Mary and, with two other young women, raced to the cover of a nearby elm. The sky exploded and lightning struck the tree!

4   Only Mary survived.

5   It was a miraculous escape. When Mary blossomed into a lively and intelligent child, some townspeople said the lightning had made her that way.

6   Mary and her older brother, Joseph, were just a few years old when they began visiting the nearby rocky beaches with their father. Richard Anning taught them how to hunt for fossils.

7   Fossils were strange and mysterious. Although they had been found before, scientists were just beginning to understand that they were the remains of animals or plants that no longer existed, living things that had died many, many years ago.

8   Usually the remains of plants and animals decompose or are eaten, but sometimes they are covered by dirt or sink in mud. Of these, a rare few lie undisturbed for millions of years. While they are buried, the soft parts, such as flesh, decay, leaving bones, shell, or flat impressions in the earth. Minerals seep into these remains and become stone. These fossils survive hidden in the ground until they are revealed by a shovel or pick, are driven to the surface by an earthquake or volcano, or are uncovered when wind or water wears away the earth.

CLOSE READ

Generate Questions

Highlight words and phrases that help you ask or answer a question about a main idea of the text.

57

Copyright © SAVVAS Learning Company LLC. All Rights Reserved.

CLOSE READ

Generate Questions

Recall a main idea that you identified in the text. Highlight sentences that help you ask or answer a question about that idea.

poverty the state of being extremely poor

9   The Annings displayed the puzzling yet delightful fossils that they found on a table near Richard's shop on Bridge Street. Wealthy tourists visiting the popular Lyme Regis shore bought them.

10   The family struggled to survive on the earnings of Richard's carpentry work, and the extra money they earned by selling fossils helped. Then Mary's father died and the family was thrown into bitter poverty.

11   Mary and Joseph still collected and sold fossils they found on the rugged ribbon of shore that separated the sea and the cliffs.

12   One day Joseph found a fantastic fossil skull. It was nearly the length of a man's arm and had a long snout that held many sharp teeth.

13   Was it a crocodile? A dragon? A monster? What did the *rest* of the creature look like?

14   A year passed before Mary discovered the answer.

15   In 1811, Mary found a fossilized skeleton beneath a cliff called Black Ven, where Joseph had found the skull. It looked like a porpoise and was about seven feet long.

16   Men helped her free the skeleton from the earth. She sold it to a rich neighbor, who showed it to scientists. They were thrilled by the rare treasure, a fossil of a reptile that had once lived in the sea. The scientists called the creature ichthyosaur, which means fish lizard. Only a few ichthyosaur fossils had ever been found and none were as nearly perfect as this one.

17   Almost everyone forgot that it had been found by twelve-year-old Mary Anning and her teenage brother.

Analyze Main Idea and Details

Underline key details that develop the text's main idea.

Analyze Main Idea and Details

Underline evidence that supports a main idea of the text.

pursued worked without stopping to get or accomplish something

18   Mary still collected fossils and also earned money from small jobs she did for her neighbors. One of them, Mrs. Stock, gave her a geology book. From it Mary learned about rocks and mountains and the earth. She read other books and taught herself about animals, fish, and fossils.

19   Years passed. When Mary was twenty years old, she and her mother and brother were still living together. They remained very poor and even sold their furniture to pay their rent.

20   Joseph became an upholsterer and Mary collected fossils alone. She made it her life's work.

21   It also must have been Mary's great delight because she pursued it despite the dangers on the rocky shore. Boulders fell from the cliffs, torrents of thick black mud slid down from the heights, high seas pummeled the shore, and waves could sweep a careless visitor away. But the beach was rich in fossils. As the cliffs crumbled, new fossils were revealed. Many were smaller than your thumb. Others were yards long and embedded in thick, heavy rock. Workers were needed to dig them from the earth, and then horses carted them away.

22   Mary sold her treasures from a small, cluttered shop on Broad Street. There she freed her latest discoveries from dirt, sand, and rock. Mary worked very carefully, sometimes for days, to avoid damaging the fossils. Sometimes she cemented a fossil to a frame to help support it. She drew pictures of them. She studied her science books.

CLOSE READ

Generate Questions

Highlight details that help you ask or answer a question about the text's main idea.

CLOSE READ

Generate Questions

Highlight evidence that demonstrates the importance of questions and answers to the main idea of the text.

23   In 1823, Mary discovered the first complete fossil of a plesiosaur, another reptile that had lived in the sea. It was an astonishing nine-foot-long creature with a long, serpentlike neck, a lizard's head, a crocodile's teeth, a chameleon's ribs, and the paddles of a whale.

24   The discovery excited scientists. Like Mary's earlier find, the ichthyosaur fossil, it was a rare clue to solving the puzzle of life long ago. What creature had become this jumble of bones trapped in rock? How did it move? What did it eat? How was it like modern creatures? Answering these questions helped reveal the ancient world in which the plesiosaur had lived.

25   Mary Anning's fame grew as people learned that she was an extraordinary fossil collector and a talented scientist. People followed her on fossil hunts. Together they plodded over the rough rocks, waded knee-deep in water, and scrambled up the cliffs to avoid the crashing waves.

26   Once Mary had to rescue a teenager, Anna Maria Pinney, from rough water. Pinney said Mary carried her with the "same ease as you would a baby."

27   William Buckland, a famous geologist, brought his family to Lyme Regis to meet Mary and to search for fossils. She escorted Buckland and his children on fossil hunts. Richard Owens, the scientist who invented the word *dinosaur*, also combed the beach with Mary.

Analyze Main Idea and Details

Underline evidence that supports a main idea about Mary Anning's life.

Vocabulary in Context

Context clues can help you determine which sense of a multiple-meaning word is being used. Use context clues to determine the meaning of *sharp* as it is used here.

Underline the context clues that support your definition.

treacherous unsafe because of hidden dangers

28   Day after day, Mary searched in the shadows of the treacherous cliffs, sometimes walking ten miles in one day. Her sharp eyes spotted fossils where others saw nothing. Mary's dog trotted faithfully beside her. People said the dog guarded her discoveries while she fetched her tools or got help.

29   During one hunt, part of a cliff collapsed. Heavy rocks crashed at Mary's feet and nearly crushed her.

30   Another time, Mary found a large fossil. She and a helper labored to recover it. The hard work blinded Mary to the rising tide that flooded the beach. Waves drenched the pair, but they saved the treasure. Later, Mary asked the man why he hadn't warned her of the rapidly flowing tide. "I was ashamed to say I was frightened when you didn't regard it," he replied.

31   In 1828, Mary discovered a very rare fossil of a pterodactyl, a flying reptile that had the body of a lizard and the snout of a crocodile. Mary's pterodactyl was displayed at the British Natural History Museum and is still there today.

32   Mary tried to make sense of her discoveries. She read her science books and studied her collection. Mary shared her ideas with the finest scientists. They prized the thoughts of the remarkable young woman who had left school when she was eleven.

33   It was said, "She knows more about the science than anyone else."

CLOSE READ

remarkable
extraordinary or outstanding

Analyze Main Idea and Details

Underline details that support an idea about the rarity of Mary Anning's fossils.

assembled put or brought together

34   By 1836, Mary had found the fossils of three ichthyosaurs, two plesiosaurs, a pterodactyl, a strange sharklike fish called Squaloraja, and an untold number of small or incomplete fossils.

35   Mary's fossil shop on Broad Street was now crowded with customers.

36   One visitor wished to record the name of the woman who had assembled such a wonderful collection. With a firm hand, Mary wrote her name in the man's notebook.

37 "I am well known throughout the whole of Europe," she said proudly.

38 Mary Anning lived from 1799 to 1847, but her spirit dwelled in a time millions of years ago, when the monsters and dragons we now call dinosaurs roamed. She had little money, but she was rich in spirit. She was unschooled, but the professors heeded her words. She rarely strayed from her home, but her name became known everywhere. Mary Anning pried fossils from the ground, but it was knowledge that she unearthed.

CLOSE READ

Generate Questions

Highlight text evidence that you can use to ask questions about how Mary Anning's work affected others.

Develop Vocabulary

In biography, authors use language that will help readers understand important events and details in a person's life. Authors may choose words with similar meanings to add variety to their writing.

My TURN Complete the graphic organizer. For each vocabulary word, write three other words with related meanings. You may use *Rare Treasure* or print and online dictionaries to help you find words.

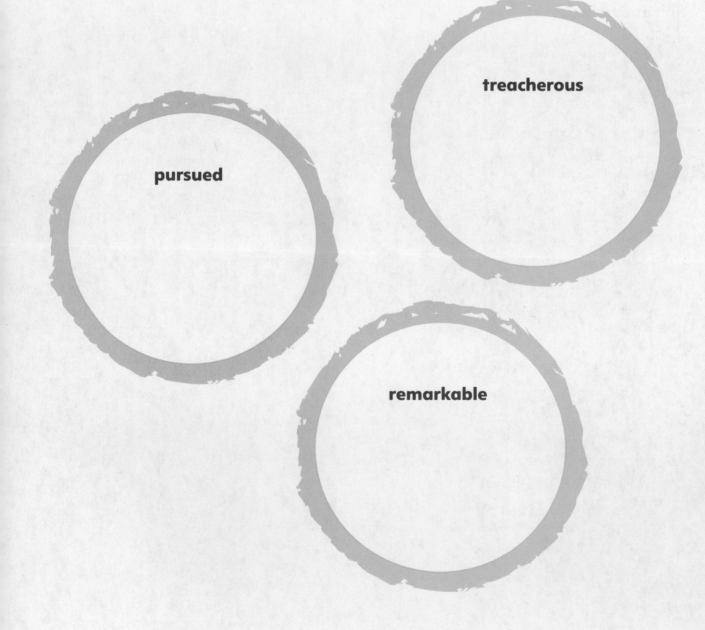

pursued

treacherous

remarkable

Check for Understanding

My TURN Look back at the text to answer the questions.

1. Name three details from the text that help you recognize it as a biography.

2. What conclusions can you draw about why Don Brown repeats the same sentence structure in the last paragraph?

3. Cite text evidence that supports the idea that collecting fossils was dangerous work.

4. Based on the title and events in the text, what connections can you make about Mary's life?

Analyze Main Idea and Details

To develop a topic, authors explore many ideas in a text, but the most important idea about a topic is called the **main idea**. Authors develop this idea by including **key details**, or pieces of supporting evidence.

1. **MyTURN** Go to the Close Read notes in *Rare Treasure* and underline key details in the text.

2. **Text Evidence** Use your evidence to write details in the chart. Then determine the main idea for *Rare Treasure*.

Main Idea

Key Detail	Key Detail	Key Detail

Generate Questions

To deepen your understanding of the text, **generate questions** before, during, and after reading. Look in the text for the answers to your questions as you read. This process will help you deepen your understanding of the main idea.

1. **My TURN** Go back to the Close Read notes. Highlight evidence that helps you generate questions about Mary Anning's work.

2. **Text Evidence** Record questions you had as you read. Then record the evidence you highlighted, and draw a conclusion about a main idea based on that evidence.

Your Questions	Evidence	Conclusion About Main Idea
What led Mary to start collecting fossils?	"Richard Anning taught them how to hunt for fossils."	After becoming interested in fossils as a child, Mary collected them throughout her life.

Reflect and Share

Write to Sources Consider all the texts you have read this week. What places did you learn about? What makes these places unique? Use these questions to write a one-sentence opinion about what makes a place special. Then use the following process to gather text evidence for an opinion paragraph.

Use Text Evidence In opinion writing, it is important to gather text evidence to support your ideas. Evidence should relate to your opinion, or claim you are making, about a topic.

Choose two texts you read this week. Choose supporting evidence from each text. Use these questions to evaluate your evidence:

- How well does this quotation support my opinion?
- How well will this quotation help me convince others?
- What quotations would make my opinion even more convincing?

After answering these questions, replace any text evidence as needed. Then, on a separate sheet of paper, use your opinion sentence and evidence to write an opinion paragraph.

Weekly Question

In what ways can a place enrich our lives?

Academic Vocabulary

A **synonym** is a word that has the same or nearly the same meaning as another word. An **antonym** is a word that means the opposite of another word.

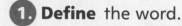 For each row in the chart,

1. **Define** the word.

2. **Choose** two synonyms and antonyms for each word.

3. **Confirm** your definitions, synonyms, and antonyms using a print or online dictionary.

contribute, *verb*	Synonyms:	Antonyms:
severe, *adjective*	Synonyms:	Antonyms:
exposed, *adjective*	Synonyms:	Antonyms:

Suffixes -ty, -ity, -ic, -ment

Suffixes are word parts added to the ends of words. Suffixes can change how words are read. The main part of the word *excitement*, *excite*, is read the same way. The ending of the main part of the word *biologic*, *biology*, is read differently. In the word *biology*, the *y* spells the sound of long *e*. When the suffix *-ic* is added, it spells the sounds short *i* and *k*.

Suffixes affect the meaning of words. For example, the word *scientific* ends with the suffix *-ic*, which means "relating to." Therefore, *scientific* means "relating to science."

My TURN Read each word and highlight the suffix. Then write the word in the correct place in the chart. Add a definition to each row. Check your definitions in a dictionary, if needed.

safety	similarity	geographic	disappointment

Suffix	Word	Definition
-ty "state of" or "quality" (noun)		
-ity "state of" or "quality" (noun)		
-ic "relating to" (adjective)		
-ment "action or process of" (noun)		

Read Like a Writer

Authors use figurative language, such as similes and metaphors, to express their ideas in inventive ways. A **simile** compares two unlike things using the comparison word *like* or *as*. A **metaphor** compares two things without using a comparison word.

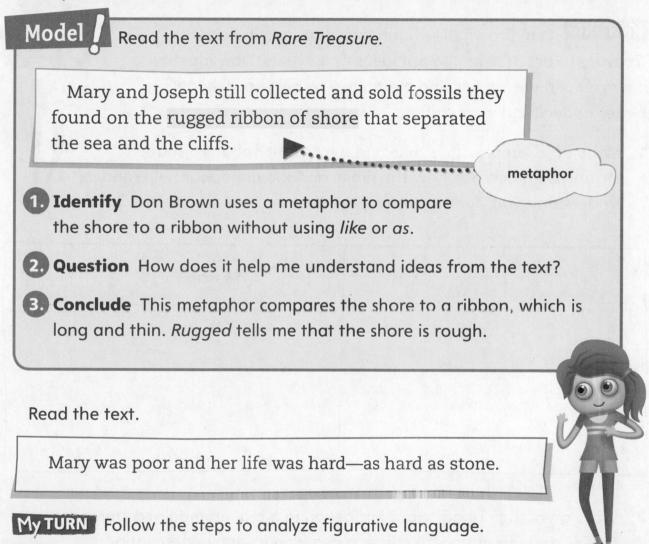

Model ! Read the text from *Rare Treasure*.

> Mary and Joseph still collected and sold fossils they found on the rugged ribbon of shore that separated the sea and the cliffs.

metaphor

1. Identify Don Brown uses a metaphor to compare the shore to a ribbon without using *like* or *as*.

2. Question How does it help me understand ideas from the text?

3. Conclude This metaphor compares the shore to a ribbon, which is long and thin. *Rugged* tells me that the shore is rough.

Read the text.

> Mary was poor and her life was hard—as hard as stone.

My TURN Follow the steps to analyze figurative language.

1. Identify This passage contains a _____ .

2. Question How does it help me understand ideas from the text?

3. Conclude This _____ compares _____ to _____ . It helps me understand _____

_____

Write for a Reader

Make your language vivid and unique!

Authors use elements of craft, such as figurative language, to describe ideas. This language may include **similes**, which compare two unlike things using *like* or *as*, or **metaphors**, which compare two things without using a comparison word.

My TURN Don Brown uses figurative language in *Rare Treasure* to describe important ideas and events. Now identify how you can use similes and metaphors to help your readers better understand your writing.

1. Write an example of a simile and a metaphor about a sudden storm. Then describe how the simile and the metaphor help readers understand your feelings during the storm.

Simile	Metaphor

2. Write a passage about what happened in a real or imagined storm. Use similes and metaphors to create a new and inventive description.

_____

_____

_____

_____

_____

Spell Words with Suffixes

Suffixes are word parts added to the end of a word. With some words, drop the final *e* before adding a suffix. For example, when you add *-ic* to *hero*, you do not have to change the spelling to make the word *heroic*. You must drop the *e* in *festive* before adding the suffix *-ity* to spell the word *festivity*.

My TURN Read the words. Then spell and alphabetize the words. Make sure to spell each word with a suffix correctly.

SPELLING WORDS

base	basic	able	ability
festive	festivity	management	loyalty
safety	commune	community	payment
enjoyment	amusement	microscope	microscopic
creative	creativity	majesty	economic

_____   _____

_____   _____

_____   _____

_____   _____

_____   _____

_____   _____

_____   _____

_____   _____

My TURN When you edit your writing, make sure to correctly use and spell words with suffixes.

Compound Subjects and Predicates

A sentence has two parts: the **subject** and the **predicate**. A simple subject is the noun or pronoun telling who or what the sentence is about. A **compound subject** is made up of two or more simple subjects joined by a conjunction, such as *and*. A simple predicate is the main verb, which tells what the subject is or does. A **compound predicate** is made up of two or more simple predicates joined by a conjunction.

Simple Subjects	Conjunction	Compound Subject
Mary removed long, embedded fossils from the heavy rock. Her **workers** removed long, embedded fossils from the heavy rock.	and	<u>Mary and her workers</u> removed long, embedded fossils from the heavy rock.

Simple Predicates	Conjunction	Compound Predicate
Mary carefully **combed** the beach. Mary **dug** endlessly for fossils.	and	Mary <u>carefully **combed** the beach and **dug** endlessly for fossils</u>.

My TURN Edit this draft by changing two simple subjects to a compound subject and two simple predicates to a compound predicate.

> Mary learned to hunt for fossils. Her brother, Joseph, learned to hunt for fossils. They used a shovel to dig for the fossils. They found where the wind or water uncovered the fossils.

Portray People

In a personal narrative, the narrator is the writer who tells the story of a personal experience. The narrator uses first-person pronouns, such as *I*, *me*, *my*, and *mine*. He or she reveals thoughts and feelings through dialogue and descriptive details.

My TURN Read a personal narrative from your classroom library. In the graphic organizer, summarize what you learned about the narrator.

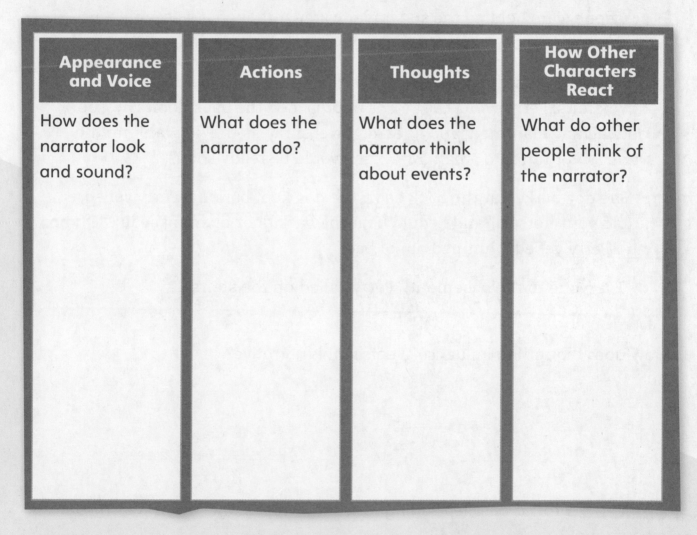

Appearance and Voice	Actions	Thoughts	How Other Characters React
How does the narrator look and sound?	What does the narrator do?	What does the narrator think about events?	What do other people think of the narrator?

My TURN In your writing notebook, use these questions to describe the narrator in your personal narrative.

Compose a Setting

The **setting** is the time and place a narrative occurs. Details reveal how the setting sounds, looks, smells, and feels. The narrator may use details to reveal the time of day and the time of year. The setting can influence what happens in a narrative.

My TURN Read the following paragraphs from a personal narrative. Underline details of the setting. Then answer the question.

> I woke up early that day. The light outside was a weird yellow, as if someone were holding the sun under water. Although it was spring, no birds were singing. I wondered if maybe I was dreaming.
>
> While I lay staring at the ceiling in the weird light, the dog whined downstairs. Perry's shuffling steps approached the back door. The door opened and slammed, and I heard gravel spray as the dog ran into the yard. Water ran into a pan. Breakfast would be ready soon.
>
> The dog barked at the back door. The dog kept barking. Perry yelled, "Hold your horses!" and I could hear the back door opening again. "Oh no, no!" Perry yelled. I jumped out of bed.
>
> "Everyone to the basement!" Perry called up the stairs.

How does the setting influence events in this narrative?

_____

_____

_____

My TURN Draft a detailed setting for your own personal narrative on your own paper.

Develop an Idea with Relevant Details

Well-structured personal narratives develop from an **engaging idea**. An idea is engaging if it interests an audience. The writer makes the idea interesting by including relevant details. A **relevant detail** relates directly to the events, setting, or people in the narrative. A detail is not relevant if it distracts readers from the setting, people, and events.

Engaging Idea	Detail	Why It Is Relevant
The school needs money to buy a new aquarium for its science classroom.	Students want to hold a car wash.	Students, including the narrator, have a chance to help solve a problem.
	None of the students know how to hold a car wash.	Someone has to take charge to solve the problem.
	The narrator's uncles operate a car wash.	The narrator has an opportunity to help solve the problem.

My TURN Read this paragraph from a personal narrative. To improve the paragraph's structure, cross out details that are not relevant.

The dance class was my mom's idea. She wanted me to explore a new hobby. Tuesday we always have spaghetti. So I went to the class on Tuesday and was worried I would be bored. Was I surprised! Instead of being boring, like an afternoon with nothing to do, the class was amazing.

My TURN Make the idea in one of your own drafts more engaging by adding relevant details to help develop a person, a setting, or an event.

Use Concrete Words and Phrases

Writers compose a personal narrative with concrete words and phrases to bring details of the setting, people, and events to life. Concrete words and phrases

◎ are **specific** instead of general.

He drove a car.　➔　He drove the **red** car.

◎ refer to **things that can be touched**.

I like coziness.　➔　I like **a wool blanket**.

◎ are **precise**.

It was the middle of the night.　➔　It was **2:00 a.m.**

My TURN Revise each sentence to make general words and phrases concrete.

1. The train was loud.

The shrieking train whistle made me jump.

2. Soup filled the bowl.

3. I feel better.

4. There will be fruit for breakfast.

Concrete words and phrases create a picture.

My TURN On one of your own drafts, add concrete details and revise general details to make them more concrete.

Compose with Sensory Details

Sensory details help the reader see, hear, taste, touch, or smell the event, people, animals, or objects you describe. Sensory details in a personal narrative let readers share the narrator's experiences. Recounting details aloud can help organize and focus your writing.

My TURN Read these paragraphs. List five sensory details, and tell what each one describes. Share your chart with members of your Writing Club.

> The library is a small place, with one bookcase of new books near the checkout counter and two rooms with old books on shelves. The old books have a musty smell, but their pages are soft. Sometimes a smudge or a streak reminds you that many other people have read the same book.
>
> "May I help you?" the white-haired man asked. I could taste that my breath was still minty. I pushed my glasses up on my nose. Then I said, "I want to apply for a job."

Sense	Sensory Detail	What It Describes
Sight		
Hearing		
Taste		
Touch		
Smell		

My TURN On one of your own drafts, add sensory details to help readers see, hear, taste, touch, or smell something you describe. Use sensory details as you describe the events aloud to your Writing Club.

INTERACTIVITY

EVERYDAY
Space Technology

Space exploration has changed our lives. Many everyday items we use on Earth were invented by NASA scientists. They had to find ways to solve problems related to traveling in space. View the media to see some examples. These inventions are made for living in space but can also help keep us safe here on Earth!

NASA developed special suits that could protect against extreme temperatures in space. Firefighters use similar suits today.

▶ Watch

NASA scientists wanted to improve comfort and safety for pilots, so they invented memory foam. Now it is used in many products, including mattresses, pillows, and amusement park rides.

NASA needed to make glasses that blocked out blue and ultraviolet light, which can damage eyes. Thanks to this technology, sunglasses are more protective than ever!

NASA needed to create small, lightweight image sensors to use on spacecraft. Those sensors led to the development of the cell phone camera.

Weekly Question

What can living in outer space teach us about the human body?

Quick Write What personal connections can you make to space technologies? Write or draw more examples of how we can use space technologies on Earth.

85

Magazine Article

A **magazine article** is a type of informational text. The author uses facts, descriptive details, and graphic features such as photographs to inform readers about a topic. Articles are often published in print and online magazines.

The author chooses a **text structure**, or way of organizing ideas, that best fits the article's purpose, audience, and content. Types of text structures include:

- **Chronological:** presents events in time order
- **Comparison-and-contrast:** describes the similarities and differences between two events, people, or ideas
- **Cause-and-effect:** identifies effects and possible causes for each event

How is a magazine article different from narrative nonfiction?

TURNandTALK With a partner, compare and contrast genres. How are *magazine articles* and *narrative nonfiction* similar? How are they different? Take notes on your discussion.

My NOTES

_____

_____

_____

_____

_____

Magazine Article Anchor Chart

Purpose:
To inform readers about a topic, often a current event

Location:
- In a print or online publication
- With other articles appealing to the same audience

Elements
- Headings that divide the text into sections

- Answers the questions

Who? What? Why? When? Where? How?

- May include interviews and research by the author

Text Structure:
- Best fits the article's purpose, audience, and content

Rebecca Boyle grew up in Colorado, which she's proud to say "is a mile closer to space." As an award-winning science writer, she investigates discoveries in astronomy, medicine, robotics, and other fascinating fields. She enjoys figuring out "how complicated things work" and exploring the world (and beyond) through her writing.

Twins in Space

Preview Vocabulary

As you read "Twins in Space," pay attention to these vocabulary words. Notice how they give clues to the ideas and structure of the text.

identical	radiation	duplicate
comparison	DNA	chromosomes

Read

Before you begin, establish a purpose for reading. Active readers of **magazine articles** follow these strategies when they read a text the first time.

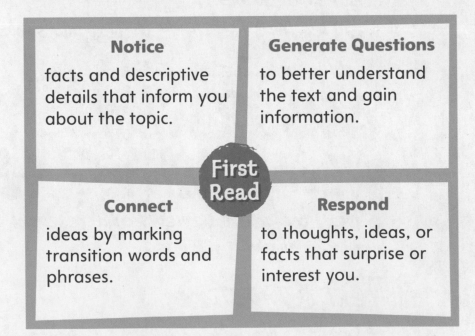

Notice
facts and descriptive details that inform you about the topic.

Generate Questions
to better understand the text and gain information.

First Read

Connect
ideas by marking transition words and phrases.

Respond
to thoughts, ideas, or facts that surprise or interest you.

TWINS IN SPACE

Can twin astronauts help us get to Mars?

by Rebecca Boyle

AUDIO

ANNOTATE

Vocabulary in Context

Context clues are words and phrases that help you understand other words in a text.

Underline context clues that help you understand the meaning of the word *envious*.

identical appearing to be exactly the same

1   One day at breakfast, Mark Kelly couldn't resist sharing his food with his identical twin brother, Scott. He couldn't really share it because Scott was too far away, so he sent his brother a picture.

2   "Sometimes when he sends me pictures of his breakfast I'm a little envious," Scott said in reply. But he knew his brother was just teasing him. Why would Scott feel jealous about breakfast? Because you can't get hot, fresh toast in space.

Up and Down

3   Scott is the commander of the International Space Station (ISS), where he has been living for a year. His twin, Mark, is also an astronaut, but has spent the last year on Earth.

Astronaut
Mark Kelly

4   Mark eats regular Earth food, exercises outside, and lives his life as usual. Scott only gets fresh food when cargo ships bring it to space. He can only exercise on a special zero-gravity treadmill and can't go outside without a spacesuit. There are other differences too. Up in space, Scott gets zapped with more energetic radiation than Mark. And of course, Scott floats around instead of walking.

5   NASA is studying everything that happens to both twins during the year, with the goal of finding out how living in space affects the human body. They already know that astronauts often get headaches, their eyesight changes, their bones and muscles get weak, and they are more likely to get sick. Scientists wonder whether staying in space longer makes these problems worse. The twins are helping them answer these questions. And that will help prepare future astronauts for long missions to Mars or other distant places.

CLOSE READ

Analyze Text Structure

Underline the main idea that is developed in the text.

radiation energy that travels in the form of waves outward from a source, such as the sun

Astronaut
Scott Kelly

Highlight the
information that is
most important to
understanding the
purpose of the NASA
study.

duplicate exactly the
same as another

comparison
examination of things to
see how they are similar

DNA the substance in
cells that determines the
characteristics of a living
thing

Duplicate Astronauts

6   The twins came up with the idea after Scott was
chosen for NASA's one-year ISS mission. The brothers
asked NASA how they should answer questions about
having a twin who is also an astronaut, and NASA
spotted a rare chance to do research.

7   Space flight affects everyone a little differently. And
every person's health is different. So how can you tell
which changes in health are caused by being in space,
and which would have happened anyway? It would
help if you could make a copy of your astronaut to stay
on the ground, as a comparison. Call in the twins!

8   Scott and Mark are identical, so they share the same
DNA. They are also both astronauts, so their overall
health and training is pretty similar. But how different
will Scott be after a year in space?

From the International
Space Station, Scott has
a great view of Earth—
and 15 sunrises a day.

9 As Susan Bailey, a scientist at Colorado State University who is studying the twins, puts it: "Because they are identical, or at least as identical as people get, we can say that any difference we see between the twins is not due to differences in their DNA, but what spaceflight has actually done to the human body. That's why the twins are so important."

Analyze Text Structure

Underline evidence in paragraphs 8–10 that helps you understand similarities and differences that support the main idea.

10 To help Bailey study those differences, the brothers give themselves medical tests at the same time. They measure themselves every day and give regular blood and other waste samples. Scott's samples get sent to Earth on supply shuttles and are flown to a lab in Colorado, where they are analyzed and compared to Mark's.

Scott's space on the ISS is cozy. Bungee cords and Velcro keep his stuff from floating around.

Evaluate Details

Highlight the information that is most important to understanding how Scott and Mark are different from other sets of twins.

A Dream Job

11   Giving samples might not be the first thing that comes to mind when you think about astronauts, but it's part of the job—and it's a job the Kelly brothers both wanted since they were little kids. Scott and Mark remember watching the 1969 Apollo 11 moon landing when they were five years old and plotting to build their own rocket. Eventually, they both joined the navy and became test pilots. They both applied to NASA in 1995 and were chosen as astronauts the following year.

12   They are the only pair of twins to both fly in space, but they have never been in space at the same time. And they've never switched places—although on the day Scott blasted off for the International Space Station, Mark couldn't resist a little joke. He shaved off his mustache and startled the flight controllers when he walked in looking like Scott, who does not have a mustache.

13   "He fooled all of us," NASA chief Charles Bolden told Scott in a phone call later. "That's the only way I can tell you two apart."

14   They both say they don't compete with each other, but they do tease each other a little bit. For instance, Mark likes to point out that he's the older brother—by just six minutes.

15   But when his year in space is up, Scott's body will probably seem older, just because spaceflight is so stressful.

CLOSE READ

Analyze Text Structure

Underline evidence that signals the text's structure.

Hands-free snacking is fun in zero G—but going outside takes some serious preparation. Notice the "Speed limit 17500" sign? That's how fast the ISS is going as it orbits Earth.

Analyze Text Structure

Underline details that explain why scientists are studying the contrasts between the twins.

chromosomes parts of DNA in cells that contain the genes

My Older Younger Brother

16 Bailey is especially interested in bundles of DNA called chromosomes. A chromosome looks like an X or Y made of a long twisted-up string of DNA. Caps at the ends of the arms are called telomeres.

17 Every time a cell divides, the telomeres get a little shorter. Eventually, there is no cap left, and that individual cell will die. Your body is replacing worn-out cells all the time, but when they wear out too quickly, it can cause health problems.

18 Radiation and stress can shorten telomeres too, Bailey says. And astronauts experience both.

19 "Imagine strapping yourself to a rocket, launching yourself to space, and staying there for a year," she says. "The isolation, the physical stresses, the emotional stresses, and the radiation exposure, all the things we don't get here on Earth."

Telomeres (colored red) are caps at the ends of chromosomes, tiny bundles of DNA inside cells. Telomeres get shorter every time a cell divides.

20   When she looks at Scott's blood, she expects to see his telomeres getting shorter at a faster rate than his brother's. That means that the stress of space is aging Scott more rapidly than Mark.

21   Bailey's study is just one of many. Scientists are also comparing the helpful bacteria that live inside the brothers' stomachs, to see how these microbes change in space. Another study will give the twins the same flu shot and compare how their bodies react to it. Yet another looks at how their vision changes over time. At the end of the year, the astronaut twins "will be the most studied people on or off the planet," Bailey says.

CLOSE READ

Evaluate Details

Highlight important comparisons of the twins that are being made in other studies.

Identical, Mostly

All through your life, what you eat and do can change which bits of DNA instructions (or genes) are switched off or on inside cells. Radiation and stress can also change DNA. As twins get older, they get less alike—though they are still more alike than other people.

Underline words and phrases that help you understand how the heading **Home and Away** relates to the way Rebecca Boyle organized the text in paragraphs 22–24.

Home and Away

22   Although spaceflight can be stressful, Scott says the astronauts have a comfortable home on the International Space Station. When he's not busy doing spacewalks or working on science experiments, he takes photos of Earth, writes emails to his family and friends, and watches football. When he misses Earth, sometimes he and the other astronauts play recordings of birds, rain, and other sounds. He misses his family and friends, but he really misses going outside, he says.

Australia looks glorious from the station window.

23 "This is a very closed environment. We can never leave. The lighting is always pretty much the same. The smells, the sounds, everything is the same," he says. "Even most prisoners can get outside occasionally, I think. But we can't. And that's what I miss, after people."

24 And hot breakfast too.

The green glow is the Northern Lights, a rain of energetic particles from the sun colliding with gas in the upper atmosphere.

Develop Vocabulary

In "Twins in Space," Rebecca Boyle uses domain-specific vocabulary to help readers understand the scientific ideas she describes.

My TURN Complete the word web. Use a print or digital dictionary to define the scientific vocabulary word in each circle. Then write a sentence using the word.

DNA
Definition:

Example Sentence:

chromosomes
Definition:

Example Sentence:

Domain: Science

duplicate
Definition:

Example Sentence:

radiation
Definition:

Example Sentence:

Check for Understanding

My TURN Look back at the texts to answer the questions.

1. How is a magazine article different from a narrative nonfiction text? Include examples from "Twins in Space" and *Rare Treasure*.

2. Explain the author's purpose in "Twins in Space." How does the "My Older Younger Brother" section support that purpose?

3. Cite two pieces of text evidence that describe why scientists want to study identical twins.

4. Based on what you read in "Twins in Space," analyze what scientists still need to learn about space travel.

Analyze Text Structure

Text structure refers to the way the author organizes the text. Authors may use more than one text structure to organize information and ideas. In "Twins in Space," Rebecca Boyle uses comparison-and-contrast text structure to describe the NASA study of the Kelly twins.

1. **My TURN** Go to the Close Read notes in "Twins in Space." Use what you underlined to determine how Rebecca Boyle supports her main idea with comparing and contrasting details.

2. **Text Evidence** Use the parts you underlined to complete the chart.

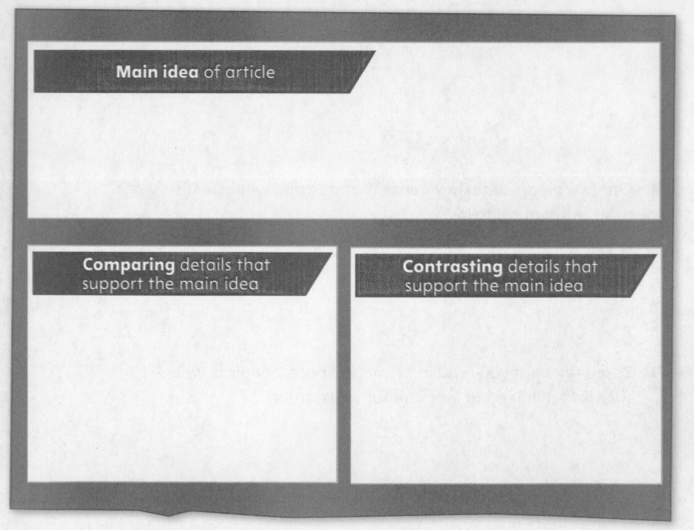

Main idea of article

Comparing details that support the main idea

Contrasting details that support the main idea

Evaluate Details

Readers can recognize the main idea in informational text by asking themselves what the text is mostly about. They can find and **evaluate details**, or supporting evidence, to form key ideas about the topic.

1. **My TURN** Go back to the Close Read notes and highlight evidence that best relates to the main idea.

2. **Text Evidence** Record the parts you highlighted in the graphic organizer. Then evaluate each detail, or piece of supporting evidence, and explain why it is important for understanding the main idea.

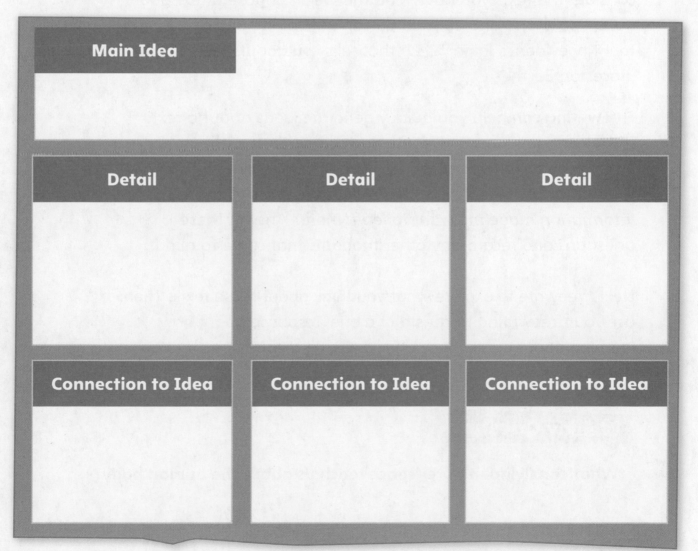

Main Idea

Detail	Detail	Detail

Connection to Idea	Connection to Idea	Connection to Idea

Reflect and Share

Write to Sources As more people study outer space, like the scientists in "Twins in Space," we learn more about our universe and even ourselves.

How has learning more about outer space affected what it means to be human? Use the following process to write and support a response.

- -

Interact with Sources For many writers, a fact or idea can inspire further research and reflection. For your response, consider the texts you have read this week. Choose a text about outer space and one about a person's life or life on Earth. Identify evidence in each text that tells you about outer space or places on Earth.

Freewriting can help you quickly generate ideas about a text. In freewriting, you simply write down your ideas without editing them. To get started, ask yourself questions, such as *What interesting facts did I learn about outer space?* or *What information made me want to learn more?* Answer these questions and record any other thoughts that come to mind.

Next, freewrite to explore what you think about these texts. Then, use your freewriting to construct a brief response about how learning about outer space affects what it means to be human.

- -

Weekly Question

What can living in outer space teach us about the human body?

Academic Vocabulary

Learning Goal

I can develop knowledge about language to make connections between reading and writing.

Context clues are words and phrases in a sentence or surrounding sentences that help you determine the meaning of unfamiliar words.

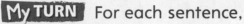 **My TURN** For each sentence,

1. **Underline** the academic vocabulary word.

2. **Highlight** the context clue or clues.

3. **Write** a definition of the word based on the clues.

One of Diya's habits is to brush her teeth every morning and every night.

Definition: _____

The archaeologist carefully chipped away at the plaster. Eventually he exposed the artifact that was underneath.

Definition: _____

By working together, all players contributed to the overall success of the team.

Definition: _____

The weather report showed signs of a severe storm, which might include a dangerous combination of sleet and strong winds.

Definition: _____

The museum placed significant value on its collection of rare Egyptian art.

Definition: _____

Syllable Pattern VCe

The **syllable pattern VCe** contains a vowel, a consonant, and the letter e. The vowel in the VCe pattern is often a long vowel sound, and the e is silent.

The word *outside* in paragraph 23 of "Twins in Space" ends with a VCe pattern. The *i* in *outside* has a long *i* sound, but the *e* is silent because of this pattern.

My TURN Read the paragraph from "Twins in Space." Then read and underline all words that have the VCe pattern with a long vowel sound.

> They are the only pair of twins to both fly in space, but they have never been in space at the same time. And they've never switched places—although on the day Scott blasted off for the International Space Station, Mark couldn't resist a little joke. He shaved off his mustache and startled the flight controllers when he walked in looking like Scott, who does not have a mustache.

Write a sentence with two of the words you underlined.

Read Like a Writer

Comparison-and-contrast text structure shows similarities and differences between two events, ideas, people, or things. Some comparing words include *also*, *both*, and *same*. Contrasting words include *but*, *however*, and *different*.

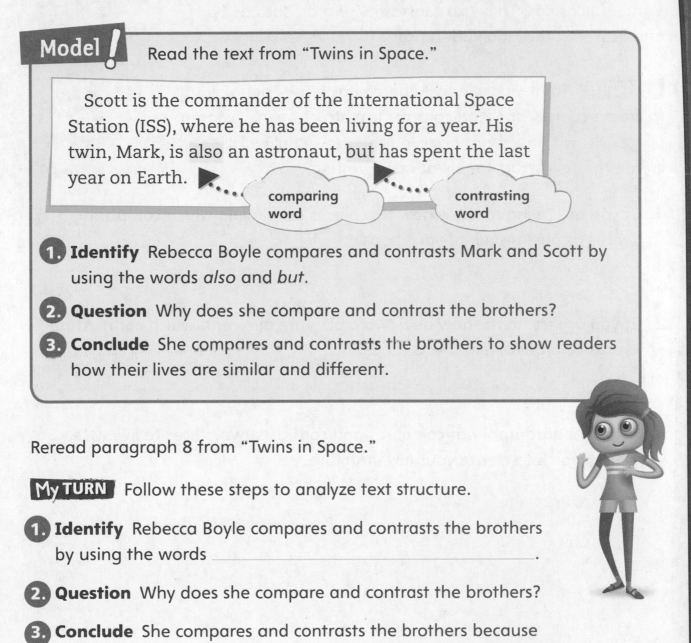

Model! Read the text from "Twins in Space."

Scott is the commander of the International Space Station (ISS), where he has been living for a year. His twin, Mark, is also an astronaut, but has spent the last year on Earth.

comparing word

contrasting word

1. **Identify** Rebecca Boyle compares and contrasts Mark and Scott by using the words *also* and *but*.

2. **Question** Why does she compare and contrast the brothers?

3. **Conclude** She compares and contrasts the brothers to show readers how their lives are similar and different.

Reread paragraph 8 from "Twins in Space."

My TURN Follow these steps to analyze text structure.

1. **Identify** Rebecca Boyle compares and contrasts the brothers by using the words _____.

2. **Question** Why does she compare and contrast the brothers?

3. **Conclude** She compares and contrasts the brothers because

_____

_____

Write for a Reader

Use comparing words to explain how two ideas or concepts are similar.

Authors use signal words to help create a specific text structure. For comparison-and-contrast text structure, authors use comparing words, such as *also* and *both*, to signal similarities. They use contrasting words, such as *but* and *however*, to signal differences.

My TURN Think about how Rebecca Boyle uses signal words to create comparison-and-contrast text structure in "Twins in Space." Now think about how you can use signal words to create this text structure in your own writing.

1. If you are trying to show how two places are similar, which **comparing** words or phrases might you choose?

   _____

2. If you are trying to show how two places are different, which **contrasting** words or phrases might you choose?

   _____

3. Write a paragraph that compares and contrasts two places to live. Use signal words to create your text structure.

   _____

   _____

   _____

   _____

   _____

   _____

   _____

Spell Words with the VCe Pattern

In words with the VCe pattern, the vowel has a long vowel sound and the e is silent. When spelling these words, be sure to include the silent e at the end.

My TURN   Sort and spell the multisyllabic words by the long vowel sound that appears in each VCe pattern.

SPELLING WORDS			
educate	fascinate	imitate	advertise
supervise	criticize	impose	corrode
cyclone	envelope	contribute	ridicule
distribute	module	episode	cooperate
participate	survive	acquire	recognize

long _a_

_____

_____

_____

_____

long _i_

_____

_____

_____

_____

long _o_

_____

_____

_____

long _u_

_____

_____

_____

Complete Sentences

Complete sentences have a subject and a predicate. A **fragment** is a group of words missing a subject or a predicate. To fix a fragment, add the missing part.

> **Fragment:** Joined the navy.
>
> **Add the missing subject:** The brothers joined the navy.

A **run-on sentence** incorrectly joins two or more sentences. To fix a run-on, separate the sentences with a period to create two sentences. You can also use a comma and a coordinating conjunction to create a compound sentence. Common coordinating conjunctions are *and*, *but*, *or*, and *yet*.

> **Run-on:** The telomeres get shorter when a cell divides soon the cell will die.
>
> **Separate sentences with a period:** The telomeres get shorter when a cell divides. Soon the cell will die.
>
> **Use a comma and a coordinating conjunction:** The telomeres get shorter when a cell divides, and soon the cell will die.

My TURN Edit the draft by fixing the fragments and run-on sentences.

> After reading "Twins in Space," I think being an astronaut is very hard you cannot go outside, and you can only eat fresh food. When it is delivered by cargo ship. You can conduct experiments you can help people learn more about life in outer space.

Develop and Compose an Introduction

Learning Goal

I can use elements of narrative nonfiction writing to write a personal narrative.

Well-organized personal narratives begin with an introduction that gives readers background. In a paragraph or two, this beginning introduces the narrator, the setting, and the situation.

- **In a personal narrative, the narrator is the writer.** Readers need to know who the writer is and why he or she is going to tell about this experience.

- **The setting is the time and the place.** Readers need to know when and where the experience took place.

- **The situation is a problem the narrator faces.** It sets events of the personal narrative in motion. Readers need to know how the situation came about and how it caused the writer's experience.

My TURN In your writing notebook, compose the introduction of your personal narrative. Use this checklist as a guide.

The introduction tells readers

☐ where the narrator is.

☐ why the narrator is writing about this experience.

☐ where and when the experience began.

☐ what problem the narrator faced.

☐ how the problem came about.

Compose an Event Sequence

A personal narrative tells about a writer's real experience through events told in order. It tells events in order so readers understand what happens first, next, and last.

A sequence of events should lead readers through the writer's experiences to the turning point of the narrative. The sequence does not have to include every detail of what happened. The writer chooses which events will tell readers the most about the experience.

My TURN Number the events to put them in the proper sequence. Put an X in front of any event that is not needed.

_____ In June, the zoo plans to open a new polar bear exhibit.

_____ My family discussed going to Alaska next summer.

_____ We decided to go to the zoo instead of to Alaska.

_____ The next day, I saw an announcement about our zoo.

_____ In geography class we are studying Russia.

_____ Bobcats live in the woods near our town.

_____ I showed the announcement to my parents.

The main events in a personal narrative lead to the turning point and cause the narrator to change.

My TURN In your writing notebook, organize an event sequence for your own personal narrative.

Use Transition Words and Phrases

Time-order and cause-and-effect transition words and phrases create structure and guide readers through the sequence of events in a personal narrative. Use time-order transitions to make the order of events clear. Use cause-and-effect transitions to explain why something happens.

Time Order		Cause-and-Effect	
before	after	therefore	as a result
first	as soon as	because	the reason
next	in the end	so	in order to
then		why	

My TURN Choose a transition word or phrase for each blank in the following paragraph.

I needed a project for my science class. _____, I asked my brother to help me find an idea. _____, we talked about my interests. _____ that, my brother said he thought making a model boat would be best, _____ I like boats more than cars. _____, I settled on making a model sailboat.

My TURN Include transitions in one of your own drafts to add structure to your piece and to clarify the sequence of events.

Compose Dialogue

Dialogue is written conversation. Writers use dialogue to show how people respond to situations or events and to each other. In dialogue, a person's words are called direct speech. Follow these rules when writing dialogue.

Rule	Example
Use quotation marks at the beginning and end of each speaker's words.	"I am making a book of my drawings."
Begin a new line whenever the speaker changes.	During art class, Juan said, "Bob, please come over here." "OK," **said Bob**. "What do you need?"
When a quotation begins in the middle of a sentence, put a comma before the quotation starts.	Juan said, "I am having trouble getting the hole punch to go through all the papers."
Begin a complete sentence with a capital letter.	Bob said, "**Let** me hold the paper steady." "Great idea," Juan replied.
Put punctuation that ends a quotation inside the quotation marks.	Juan squeezed the hole punch. "All right!" he cried. "Do you need anything else?" Bob asked.

My TURN Add punctuation and quotation marks to the dialogue.

Lan is a strong swimmer said Nnenna. I think she is going to win a ribbon

in this race

Sam asked What do you think, Bella?

I agree with you Bella replied.

My TURN Draft a brief dialogue you could add to your own personal narrative.

Develop and Compose a Conclusion

The turning point of a personal narrative brings about the **conclusion**, or ending. The narrator has experienced a change. A conclusion is usually one or two paragraphs long. It may contain

- A report of events that follow the turning point
- A brief summary of how the narrator changed
- The narrator's thoughts and feelings about the experience

My TURN Use this organizer when you compose the conclusion to your personal narrative in your writing notebook.

What events came after the turning point?

In one sentence, how did the experience change me?

Which thoughts and feelings do I most want my readers to know?

My TURN Identify a topic, purpose, and audience. Then select any genre, and plan a draft by brainstorming your ideas.

115

INTERACTIVITY

COOL HOMES
Around the World

IN THE RAIN FOREST Some people live in **tree houses**. A tree house like this one gives the people inside a bird's-eye view. People can see much farther than they can at ground level.

ON THE STEPPE A **yurt** is a round home made out of flexible wood and a soft material called felt. Its portability and round shape make it well suited to the wide, open spaces and strong winds of the steppe.

IN THE MOUNTAINS Log cabins were originally built with soft timber. People could easily make these homes with simple hand tools. They could be built in days using only a saw, an ax, and an auger, a type of tool that bores holes into wood.

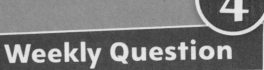
Weekly Question

What are the advantages of living in different places?

Illustrate Draw a house in the area where you live. Show details such as the materials that make the house and how the shape or location of the house relates to the environment.

IN THE ARCTIC Igloos are built with bricks that are carved from packed snow on the ground. The structures keep the cold out and keep the people inside warm. Igloos are usually temporary shelters.

Informational Text

Authors of **informational text** want to help readers learn about a topic. The purpose of the text is to *inform*. Authors do that by including facts and details. Authors may use formatting and text features to call attention to certain information or clarify relationships between ideas.

TURN and TALK What kinds of information does a map show? How does a map help you understand certain ideas? With a partner, compare and contrast the experience of reading a map to reading a paragraph about a location.

Be a Fluent Reader Reading aloud for an audience is similar in some ways to reading silently. When you read, you monitor your understanding of the text. You also read at a **rate** that is appropriate for the text.

When you read informational text aloud:

◎ Read at a rate that is slow enough to not skip words.

◎ Read at about the same speed you would normally speak.

◎ If you come to a word you do not know, you can still stop to sound it out.

INFORMATIONAL TEXT
ANCHOR CHART

Purpose:
To inform or explain

Text Features

- Pronunciation guides show how to correctly say difficult or unusual words aloud.
- Boldface words show key vocabulary.
- Headings organize information.

Visual Elements

★ Photographs and illustrations show information visually.

★ Diagrams show processes or links between information.

★ Charts, tables, and graphs show numerical data.

★ Maps show geographical locations.

Meet *the* Author

Veronica Ellis has a love of words and storytelling that began in her birthplace, Liberia. It continued through her school years in England, as well as her college years in the United States. She teaches writing at the College of Communication at Boston University. She is the author of several children's books.

Life at the Top

Preview Vocabulary

As you read *Life at the Top*, pay attention to these vocabulary words. Notice how they help you understand what you read and what you see in the text.

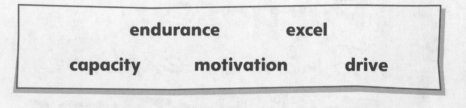

endurance	excel
capacity	motivation	drive

Read

Before you read, scan for text features. Make predictions about what you will learn in the text based on what you see. Record your predictions on a separate sheet of paper. Then follow these strategies as you read this **informational text** for the first time.

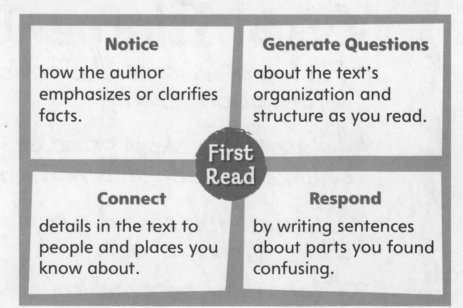

Notice how the author emphasizes or clarifies facts.

Generate Questions about the text's organization and structure as you read.

First Read

Connect details in the text to people and places you know about.

Respond by writing sentences about parts you found confusing.

Life at the Top

by Veronica Ellis

AUDIO

ANNOTATE

Analyze Text Features

<u>Underline</u> details in the text that are supported by the photograph and caption.

endurance the ability to keep going

1   Some people climb mountains for the challenge. Others climb for the view from the top. They may stay long enough to snap some photos, and then they turn around and climb back down. Then there's another group. These folks travel up, up, and up and then stay there—for days, weeks, or months. Or they move there permanently.

2   These are athletes who believe in the power of being at the top. They're convinced that training at high altitude—8,000 feet or more above sea level—is the key to peak sports performance. They live by the idea that altitude builds stronger hearts, more efficient lungs, and better endurance. So when these athletes go back down to sea level, they can be faster, stronger, and just plain better than those who never left sea level.

Running at High Altitude

3   Runners, in particular, are fans of training at high altitudes. These days, altitude training is part of almost all top runners' training programs. Since 1968, ninety-five percent of all runners who have won medals in world championships and the Olympic games have trained or lived at high altitude. That's enough to persuade any athlete to head for the hills!

4   Many runners attend special high-altitude training camps to prepare for marathons, the Olympics, and other races. One of the most famous of these camps is located in Kenya, Africa. It's called (unsurprisingly) the High Altitude Training Center.

CLOSE READ

Confirm or Correct Predictions

Use the photograph and the text in this section to highlight details that help you confirm a prediction you made before reading the text.

These long-distance runners are in training at the High Altitude Training Center.

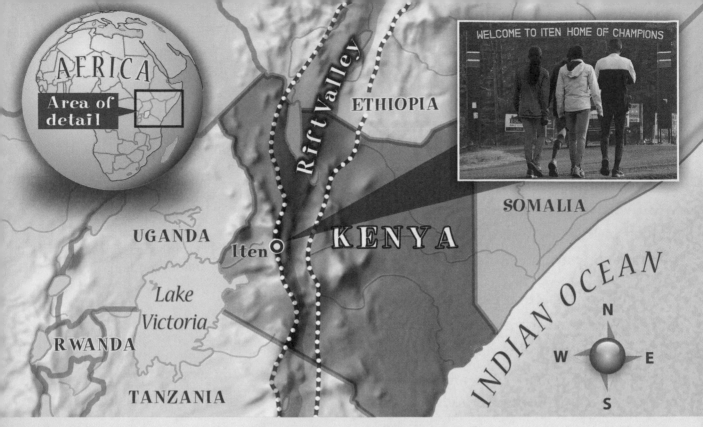

Analyze Text Features

Underline the text features that can help you pronounce key words.

5   The Center is in the village of Iten (eye TEN), on top of a steep cliff, overlooking Kenya's Great Rift Valley. At its highest spots, the Great Rift Valley is almost 7,000 feet above sea level. That's not officially "high altitude," but almost.

6   The High Altitude Training Center was founded by Lornah Kiplagat. Kiplagat is a Kenyan runner who has competed in many long-distance races around the world. She raced in the Olympics, won World Road Running Championships three times, and won a gold medal at the World Cross Country Championships. In other words, she takes running very seriously.

7   As a runner, Kiplagat has helped bring athletic fame to Kenya and to her people, the Kalenjin (kah LEN jin), who live in the Great Rift Valley. As the founder of the High Altitude Training Center, she has helped runners from around the world achieve their personal best.

8   Kiplagat founded the training center in 2000. Her goal was a simple one. She wanted to give other Kenyan girls and women the chance to train and excel.

9   For Kiplagat, deciding to create her running camp in the high-altitude town of Iten was a no-brainer. For one thing, it's just above the place where she grew up and became a runner herself: the Great Rift Valley.

Lornah Kiplagat, wearing orange, is the champion athlete who founded the High Altitude Training Center.

Analyze Text Features

Underline a sentence that is supported by the photograph and caption.

excel do well or be the best at something

Kenyan runner Joyce Chepkirui (far right) won this 8 km race.

CLOSE READ

Analyze Text Features

Underline information in the text that is supported by text features.

Benefits of Altitude

10   Growing up and becoming a runner in the Great Rift Valley also gave Kiplagat personal experience with the benefits of training at high altitude. And Kiplagat is just one of many, many world-class runners from that region.

11 Here are some statistics to back up that claim. Kenyan journalist John Manners spent most of his career studying runners from his country. He found that Kalenjin runners such as Kiplagat won about three-quarters of all races in Kenya. Yet Kalenjins make up only 10 to 12 percent of the country's population! Another study found that Kalenjin athletes won approximately 40 percent of all major international mid- and long-distance running competitions during a 10-year period.

What Happens Up There?

12 Does living and training at high altitude contribute to these athletes' success? The runners who flock to training camps such as Kiplagat's clearly think so. But what does science say about all of this?

13 There has been a lot of research on the subject. However, scientists still don't know for sure if high-altitude training can help improve athletic performance. One thing is for sure. Your body performs differently when you are far above sea level.

14 If you've ever traveled to a high altitude, you know that it can be harder to breathe up there—at first. That's because the air pressure is lower the higher you go. When air pressure is low, air particles are farther apart. Air particles contain oxygen. So when you're higher up, you don't breathe in as many air particles. That means your body takes in less oxygen than it would at sea level.

Confirm or Correct Predictions

Use the photograph and what you have read so far to highlight details that help you confirm or correct a prediction you made about the text.

Analyze Text Features

Underline details that connect to the information in the diagram.

15   But after you've been at high altitude for a while, your body adjusts. It starts to make more red blood cells. Those are the cells that carry oxygen in the body. More red blood cells means you can breathe more easily.

16   After you've adjusted to a higher altitude, you can hike, climb, bike, or run longer up there than you could at sea level. That's because you have more oxygen in your blood. Your lungs become more efficient too. They expand more to take in more air. You breathe harder and deeper at high altitudes to take in more fresh air.

17   Spending time at high altitude can also be good for people's heart health. Scientists believe the lower oxygen level in the air may ignite, or start up, certain genes in the body. These genes cause the heart muscles to work more effectively.

18   Bodies also adapt at higher altitudes by losing weight. If you live in a high-altitude area, you'll have a lower appetite than people who live at sea level. Why? At high altitudes, your body makes more of a hormone that makes you feel full faster. As a result, you'll eat less.

19   That makes a difference for runners. Being thinner can help you run faster. To run, you move forward by jumping into the air. When you jump, you're fighting gravity. The more you weigh, the harder that is.

20   All of these benefits of high altitude may mean better athletic performance at sea level. It's not hard to understand why. Athletes who train at 8,000 feet or more have greater lung capacity, heart strength, and endurance. They can speed past someone who has been training only at sea level.

capacity the ability to contain something

Training at high altitude changes the rate at which the **heart** beats and how much blood it pushes with each heartbeat.

The capacity of **lungs** increases at high altitude, so they can take in more air at once.

High altitude training can increase blood flow to **muscles** and let them do more work before getting tired.

Analyze Text Features

Underline details in the text that support what you see in the image.

21   But how much of the Kalenjin runners' success is really due to altitude? Might other factors be involved?

22   For example, the land in the Great Rift Valley is mostly flat, and the weather is mild all year long. That means runners can train outside regularly. This is a big advantage. Of course, other places have flat land. Other places have good weather. Yet other places don't have so many great runners.

23   Some people say the Kalenjin diet helps with running speed. It's a plain diet. It includes foods such as corn, sweet potatoes, and other local crops. Their staple meal is called ugali (yoo-gah-lee), a paste usually made from cornmeal. It's often served with stewed vegetables. Although a meal like this is simple, it contains a lot of nutrients. It's also high in carbohydrates. Those give the body long-lasting energy. However, many people around the world eat similar diets. Yet they aren't winning most of the world's long-distance races!

24   Some give another explanation for Kalenjin runners' greatness. They have a very active lifestyle. Many Kalenjin families farm and herd cattle. That means they move around a lot. But again, so do people in many other parts of the world.

CLOSE READ

Confirm or Correct Predictions

Highlight details that help you confirm or correct a prediction you made about the text.

This Olympic gold medalist trains at the High Altitude Training Center.

25   People also often say that Kalenjin children run more than other children. There are many stories about children running in groups to and from school each day. According to these stories, often they run barefoot. The barefoot part is important. This is because barefoot runners touch the ground with their forefoot or midfoot. Scientists say that's less stressful than hitting the ground heel first. Less stress on the feet makes people run faster. However, these running stories may be exaggerated. Many adult Kalenjin runners report they took the bus or walked to school as children. So much for that theory.

motivation a reason for doing something

26   There are two other explanations for why the Kalenjin people produce so many great runners. One is economic. Kenya has a poor economy. By winning one marathon, a Kalenjin might earn enough to live on for an entire lifetime. That's pretty good motivation. Another related explanation is social. Mental toughness is a highly valued trait among the Kalenjin. Without it, no athlete can get far. In addition, Kalenjin runners are surrounded by other runners. That's motivating, too.

The Role of Community... and Hard Work

27   Lornah Kiplagat's High Altitude Training Center and others of its kind are built around the idea of running and achieving your best as part of a community. High-altitude training may make runners faster. However, the support of others helps many athletes keep going when they might want to quit.

28   Mary Keitany is another world-champion Kenyan runner. She trained in Iten too. Like Lornah Kiplagat, Keitany competes in and wins marathons and long-distance races around the world. She wins at high and low altitudes.

CLOSE READ

Confirm or Correct Predictions

Highlight details that help you confirm or correct a prediction about why high-altitude runners are successful.

Runner Mary Keitany broke a marathon world record in 2017.

Vocabulary in Context

Readers use context clues, or the words and sentences around an unfamiliar word, to determine the meaning of the word.

Use context clues to determine the meaning of *expanding*.

Underline the context clues that support your definition.

29   Keitany started her professional running career about a decade ago. She first won Kenya's largest women's-only race. It's called the Shoe4Africa 5K. (The organization Shoe4Africa is supported by Lornah Kiplagat and many others. It raises money for healthcare and education all over Africa.) In interviews, Keitany credits hard work, not high altitude, for her winning ways. But there's no question that for her, as for Kiplagat, working hard *at* high altitudes has produced great results.

30   These days, high-altitude training is not limited to Kenya. The trend of training up high seems to be expanding as fast as runners' lung capacity. High-altitude training centers have popped up all over. You can find them in the French Pyrenees mountain range. They're in South Africa. They're in Colorado too.

31   Effective high-altitude training requires more than just climbing to 8,000 feet, though. Trainers who believe in the power of altitude usually have a few rules to follow. For one, they say athletes should stay at high altitude for 18 to 28 days. Less than that and they won't achieve the full benefits.

32   Many trainers believe athletes need to time their training just right, too. Some experts estimate that runners who come down from altitude more than two or three weeks before a race will erase the benefits of their high-altitude training.

Edna Kiplagat won the 2017 Boston Marathon.

33   What can other athletes learn from Kalenjin runners? No doubt, the Kalenjin have geography in their favor. They have high altitude, flat land, and a mild climate. A nutrient-rich diet and active lifestyle also help.

34   Most important, perhaps, are drive and determination. When it comes down to it, the Kalenjin may not win races just because of the geography of their area. Runners hoping to improve can add high-altitude training. However, they should also pay attention to the fact that the Kalenjin might be the hardest-working runners on Earth.

CLOSE READ

drive the ambition or motivation to carry on

Fluency

Read paragraphs 33–34 aloud with a partner. Pay attention to rate as you read. Practice reading at a rate that will help your partner understand the text. You can stop to sound out words, if needed.

Develop Vocabulary

In informational texts, authors use precise words to describe important ideas about a topic. For example, in *Life at the Top*, Veronica Ellis uses *altitude* and *sea level* to describe basic ideas about how location affects a runner's body.

My TURN Read each pair of words from *Life at the Top*. Then explain how these words help you understand an idea from the text.

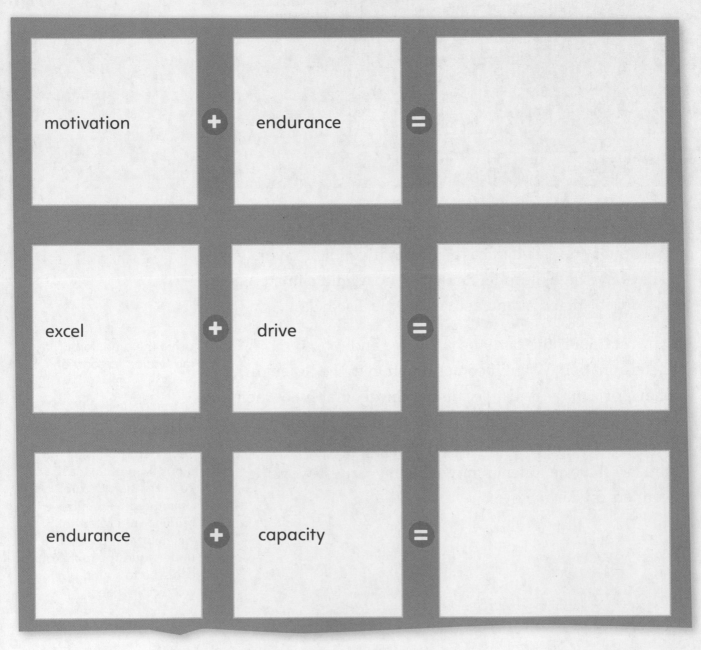

motivation   **+**   endurance   **=**

excel   **+**   drive   **=**

endurance   **+**   capacity   **=**

Check for Understanding

My TURN Look back at the text to answer the questions.

1. What characteristics of *Life at the Top* tell you it is an informational text?

2. Why do you think Veronica Ellis included a diagram? Cite text evidence and details from the diagram in your answer.

3. Based on the "Is It All About Altitude?" section, draw a conclusion about the factors that lead to the Kalenjin runners' success.

4. Which evidence from *Life at the Top* would be the most convincing in an argument about why all runners should have high-altitude training?

Analyze Text Features

Authors use **text features**, such as headings, maps, diagrams, photographs, and illustrations, to organize and support ideas in a text. By analyzing these print and graphic features, you can better understand the text.

1. **MyTURN** Go to the Close Read notes in *Life at the Top* and underline information related to the text features.

2. **Text Evidence** Use the evidence you underlined to complete the chart.

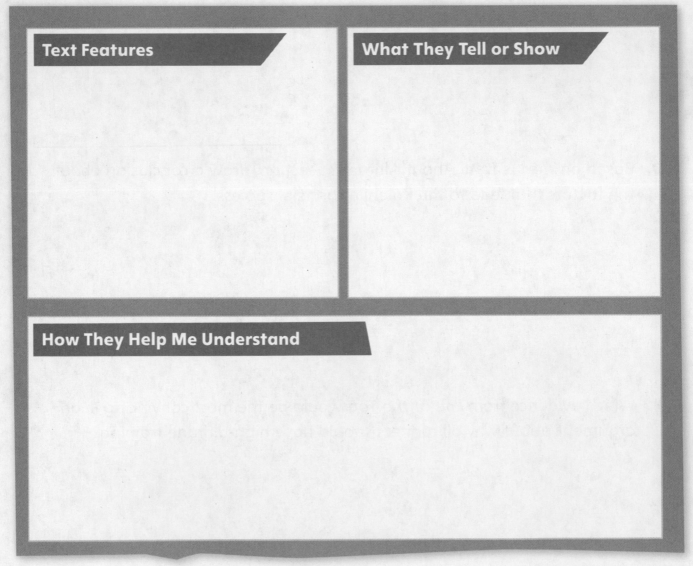

Text Features

What They Tell or Show

How They Help Me Understand

Confirm or Correct Predictions

Use the title, headings, and text features to make predictions before you read. Then confirm or correct your predictions as you read. Look for information in the text that supports, or **confirms** your prediction. Other information may help you check and **correct** your prediction.

1. **My TURN** Return to the First Read page and the predictions you made about *Life at the Top.* Then go back to the Close Read notes and highlight details that helped you confirm or correct a prediction you made.

2. **Text Evidence** Use one of your predictions and the text you highlighted to complete the graphic organizer.

Prediction

Evidence Related to My Prediction

Reflect and Share

Write to Sources In *Life at the Top*, Veronica Ellis explains the benefits athletes gain when they train at high altitudes. What other places offer advantages to the people who live there? Choose two places you read about this week. Then use examples from the texts to write and support a response.

- -

Compare and Contrast Writers may use comparison-and-contrast text structure to explore ideas in depth. They look at what is the same and what is different to help them evaluate what they think about a topic. Use a Venn diagram to take notes about the two places you chose.

Use your notes to write a response that compares and contrasts the two places you chose. Use information from the texts you read to support your ideas.

- -

Weekly Question

What are the advantages of living in different places?

Academic Vocabulary

Figurative language is any language that gives a word a meaning beyond its usual, everyday definition. One type of figurative language is a simile, which compares two things using the word *like* or *as*.

Learning Goal

I can develop knowledge about language to make connections between reading and writing.

My TURN For each sentence,

1. **Read** the sentence and underline the simile.

2. **Match** the word in the box with the simile that best relates to the definition of the word.

3. **Choose** two similes. Then use each simile and its related academic vocabulary word in a sentence.

WORD BANK

exposed   habit   severe   significant

He left the house at the same time every day like clockwork. _____

Regular exercise is as vital as blood. _____

When everyone learned the secret, it was like pulling back the curtains.

_____

Her angry expression looked like a brewing storm. _____

Vowel Teams and Digraphs

Vowel teams are two or three letters that spell one vowel sound. Some vowel teams are also called **vowel digraphs**. In vowel digraphs, often the first vowel spells a long vowel sound, and the second vowel is silent. In the multisyllabic word *teammate*, the vowel team *ea* spells the long e sound. In the word *bread*, the vowel team *ea* spells the short e sound. In the word *drain*, the vowel team *ai* spells the long *a* sound. Knowing these patterns can help you read multisyllabic words.

My TURN Use these activities to apply your knowledge of vowel teams and digraphs.

1. Read these words with vowel teams, or digraphs: *drainage, mainstay, leader, boasting, playful.*

2. Choose two words with vowel digraphs, and use each in a sentence.

_____

_____

_____

High-Frequency Words

High-frequency words are words that you see over and over again. They often do not follow regular word study patterns. Read these high-frequency words: *heart, probably, factors, beautiful, sign, discovered.* Try to identify them in your independent reading.

Read Like a Writer

Authors use print or graphic features to help readers find information. Headings organize ideas based on a common topic or concept. Photographs and other graphic features help readers visualize ideas from the text.

> **Model !** Look at the photograph near paragraphs 8 and 9 in *Life at the Top*.
>
> **1. Identify** The photograph shows Lornah Kiplagat, a woman from Kenya, running in a race.
>
> **2. Question** Why does Veronica Ellis include this text feature?
>
> **3. Conclude** Veronica Ellis uses this feature to show an example of a runner who lives at a high altitude and runs very fast.

Look at this text feature and read the text.

> ## Is It All About Altitude?
>
> But how much of the Kalenjin runners' success is really due to altitude? Might other factors be involved?

My TURN Follow the steps to analyze the author's use of a text feature.

1. Identify The heading is _____.

2. Question Why does Veronica Ellis include this text feature?

3. Conclude Veronica Ellis uses this feature to _____

_____

_____

Write for a Reader

Headings can help you organize your ideas.

Authors use print and graphic features to organize and support their ideas. They use headings to group related information. They use photographs, diagrams, and other visual elements to help readers visualize ideas from the text.

My TURN Think about Veronica Ellis's purpose for using text features in *Life at the Top*. Now think about how you use text features in your own writing.

1. If you wanted to write a paragraph about how eating well can help an athlete swim faster, what text features might you use?

2. Use the features you identified to write a passage about how an athlete's diet can affect how long and far he or she can run.

Spell Words with Vowel Teams and Digraphs

Vowel teams are usually two letters that spell one vowel sound. For example, the letters *a* and *y* are a vowel team that spell the long *a* sound in words like *stay* and *play*. Some vowel teams can also be called **vowel digraphs**.

My TURN Read the words. Then spell and alphabetize the words. Make sure to spell each vowel team correctly.

SPELLING WORDS

increase	yesterday	acquaint	achievement
reproach	marrow	virtue	continue
betray	array	campaign	revenue
meadow	deceive	appeal	agreement
streamline	proceed	remainder	straight

Fix Run-On Sentences

Run-on sentences are two complete sentences joined without correct punctuation or a conjunction. A **comma splice** is a type of run-on sentence that uses a comma to incorrectly connect two sentences without also using a conjunction. Run-on sentences can be fixed by creating two sentences. Run-on sentences can also be fixed by adding a comma and a conjunction to create a compound sentence.

Run-On Sentence	Corrected Sentence(s)
By winning one marathon, a Kalenjin might earn enough to live on for an entire lifetime that's pretty good motivation.	By winning one marathon, a Kalenjin might earn enough to live on for an entire lifetime. That's pretty good motivation.
She first won Kenya's largest women's-only race it's called the Shoe4Africa 5K.	She first won Kenya's largest women's-only race. It's called the Shoe4Africa 5K.
Runners can regularly train outside, this is a big advantage.	Runners can regularly train outside, and this is a big advantage.

My TURN Edit this draft by fixing the run-on sentences including comma splices.

Many runners use high-altitude training to prepare for races, one of the most famous training camps is in Kenya, Africa. At this camp, runners eat simple meals with foods like corn, sweet potatoes, and other local crops these foods have carbohydrates that give the body long-lasting energy.

Add Ideas for Coherence and Clarity

To make their **personal narratives** clearer, writers add ideas that

- connect events to one another
- show how people act, think, and feel

The ideas can be words, parts of sentences, or whole sentences.

My TURN Study the first paragraph to learn how the writer added ideas in blue to make the paragraph clearer. Then add details to the second paragraph to make it clearer. Choose only the most relevant details.

Detail Bank

There are height, weight, and age restrictions.

Mules are sure-footed.   **Then admire the view.**

People ride mules to get into the canyon.

The Grand Canyon was awesome. It was deeper than we had imagined. How were we going to get to the bottom?

_____ The mules know how to walk on the narrow paths that wind down. Not everyone is allowed to ride them. _____

_____

My TURN On one of your own drafts, identify ideas that may be vague or incomplete. Add details to clarify your ideas.

147

Delete Ideas for Coherence and Clarity

To make their narratives clearer, writers remove ideas that

○ are repetitive
○ do not relate to the main events or points

My TURN Read this edited paragraph. The writer has crossed out ideas to make the paragraph clearer. Write in the chart why the writer deleted each detail.

One day at the library, I found an old book ~~that I decided to read. It was~~ about the Declaration of Independence. I read about the summer of 1776, when the Declaration was written. ~~It took a while for people to sign it.~~ The book had ~~regular pages, but it also had pages of shiny paper. Those pages showed~~ paintings of people who signed the Declaration of Independence. It was very exciting to see the people who decided to declare independence.

Deleted Idea	Why It Was Deleted
First Deleted Detail Second Deleted Detail Third Deleted Detail	

My TURN On one of your own drafts, delete repetitive or unnecessary ideas.

Edit for Adjectives

An **adjective** describes a noun or pronoun, often by answering the questions *What kind? How many?* or *Which one?* A **comparative adjective** compares two nouns. A **superlative adjective** compares three or more nouns.

Rule	Comparative	Superlative	Examples
Add -*er* and -*est* to short adjectives.	softer	softest	The feather is softer than the leaf. This is the softest shirt I have.
Use *more* and *most* with long adjectives.	more experienced	most experienced	Elvio is a more experienced drummer than Ben. Kim is the most experienced drummer in the band.

Adjectives usually come before the word they describe. When you use two or more adjectives to describe one thing, put the adjectives in this order.

Farthest from noun   **Closest to noun**

opinion   **size**   **age**   **shape**   **color**
brave   *huge*   *old*   *flat*   *red*

My TURN Highlight the correct adjectives in these sentences.

The pony takes the *quickest/most quick* path through the trees back to the barn. I hope that tomorrow the pony will be *easygoinger/more easygoing* on our trail ride.

My TURN Edit one of your own drafts for correct use of comparative and superlative adjectives. Check that adjectives are in correct order.

Edit for Adverbs

Writers use adverbs to add details to their writing. **Adverbs** tell how, where, or when an action happens. Two kinds of adverbs are adverbs of frequency and adverbs of degree.

Type	Purpose	Examples	Sample Sentence
Adverb of frequency	Tells how often a verb happens	always, often, regularly, sometimes, occasionally, usually	I usually finish my homework after dinner.
Adverb of degree	Tells how strongly an adjective or another adverb applies to a situation	very, extremely, totally, quite, somewhat, slightly, completely	She feels very nervous, although she succeeds quite regularly.

A **relative adverb** connects two related clauses. A **clause** has a subject and a verb. English has three common relative adverbs: *where*, *when*, and *why*.

Clause 1	Relative Adverb	Clause 2
This is the box	where	he kept the ring.
I do not know	why	the soup is gone.

My TURN Edit the paragraph to correct each underlined adverb.

On Saturdays Maddie's mom <u>totally</u> teaches her something <u>usually</u> new about sewing. We wondered <u>when</u> Maddie left Harun's birthday party. It was because she wanted to get home on time.

My TURN Use adverbs to add concrete details to your personal narrative.

Edit for Pronouns

To add variety to your writing, use pronouns. **Pronouns** replace nouns or groups of nouns. Pronouns may be

- **subjective,** used as the subject of a sentence or clause
  They have brown eyes.

- **objective,** used as the object of a verb or a preposition
  The server handed them the menu.

- **possessive,** used to show ownership
  Swimmers stayed in their lanes.

- **reflexive,** used to reflect an action back to the subject.
  The tourists bought themselves some souvenirs.

Subjective	Objective	Possessive	Reflexive
Singular			
I	me	my, mine	myself
you	you	your	yourself
he	him	his	himself
she	her	her	herself
it	it	its	itself
Plural			
we	us	our	ourselves
you	you	your	yourselves
they	them	their	themselves

A **relative pronoun** connects two related clauses. A **clause** has a subject and a verb. English has five common relative pronouns: *who, whose, whom, which,* and *that*. A relative pronoun takes the place of a noun in the second clause.

My TURN Edit one of your own drafts to check for incorrect pronouns.

INTERACTIVITY

TAKING CARE
of Our Land

In 1872, President Ulysses S. Grant signed the National Park Protection Act into law. In doing so, he established the world's first national park.

Yellowstone Park is almost 3,500 square miles of wilderness in Montana, Wyoming, and Idaho. It is a wonder of geology with unique features, such as hot springs and gushing geysers. It is also home to wild animals, including bears, wolves, bison, elk, and pronghorn.

AN ACT TO SET APART A CERTAIN TRACT OF LAND LYING NEAR THE HEADWATERS OF THE YELLOWSTONE RIVER AS A PUBLIC PARK.

APPROVED

March 1, 1872 (17 Stat. 32)

Be it enacted by the Senate and House of Representatives of the United States of America in Congress assembled, That the tract of land in the Territories of Montana and Wyoming, lying near the headwaters of the Yellowstone River, and described as follows, . . . is hereby reserved and withdrawn from settlement, occupancy, or sale under the laws of the United States, and dedicated and set apart as a public park or pleasuring-ground for the benefit and enjoyment of the people. . . . (U.S.C., title 16, sec. 21.)

SEC 2.

That said public park shall be under the exclusive control of the Secretary of the Interior, whose duty it shall be, as soon as practicable, to make and publish such rules and regulations as he may deem necessary or proper for the care and management of the same. Such regulations shall provide for the preservation, from injury or spoliation, of all timber, mineral deposits, natural curiosities, or wonders within said park, and their retention in their natural condition.

Weekly Question

How can people influence the places where they live?

TURN and TALK Take turns reading the sections of the primary source aloud with a partner. Work together to paraphrase the text, or put it in your own words.

Natural resources are the animals, plants, and land in a place. What natural resources are near where you live? How do those resources make your community a special place to live? Take notes on your conversation.

Learning Goal

I can learn more about narrative nonfiction by analyzing text structure in a biography.

Spotlight on Genre

Biography

A **biography** is a type of narrative nonfiction that tells a person's life story or part of it. That person is called the **subject** of the biography. The subject may still be alive or may have lived in the past.

In a biography, authors often use **chronological**, or time order, **structure**. Authors use this text structure to tell the story of the subject's life. Authors often include specific dates and times to help readers understand more about the subject. For example, authors may describe a specific time period to help readers understand how the subject's life relates to events in history.

Establish Purpose The **purpose**, or reason, for reading a biography is to learn about significant events in a person's life. Narrative elements in biographies help keep readers interested.

Biographies tell stories about real people. What do you want to learn from reading a biography?

> **My PURPOSE** _____
> _____
> _____
> _____
>
> **TURN and TALK** With a partner, establish a purpose for reading *Barbed Wire Baseball*. Talk about how this purpose will affect your plan for reading.

CHRONOLOGICAL ORDER

- Also called time order
- Tells events in order in which they happened
- Can be used in many genres, including fiction, autobiography, biography and informational texts
- Usually includes signal words, or transitions, to show events in order

CHRONOLOGICAL ORDER TRANSITIONS

FIRST	LATER	IN THE BEGINNING
NEXT	EVENTUALLY	AFTER SOME TIME
THEN	FINALLY	IN A WHILE

Marissa Moss has always been enthusiastic about writing. She sent her first book to publishers when she was just nine years old! Marissa Moss has written more than forty books for children and especially enjoys writing about history. She loves how historical sources "can make a strange, vague period of the past seem vivid and familiar."

Barbed Wire Baseball

Preview Vocabulary

Read the list of words. Then look at the cover of *Barbed Wire Baseball*. What do you predict this selection will be about? Pay attention to the vocabulary words as you read the text.

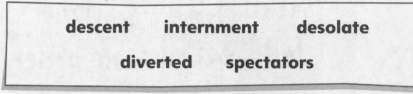

descent	internment	desolate
	diverted	spectators

Read

Active readers of **biographies** follow these strategies when they read a text the first time.

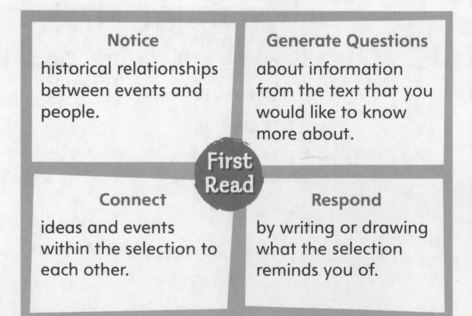

Notice historical relationships between events and people.

Generate Questions about information from the text that you would like to know more about.

First Read

Connect ideas and events within the selection to each other.

Respond by writing or drawing what the selection reminds you of.

Barbed Wire BASEBALL

by Marissa Moss
illustrated by Yuko Shimizu

AUDIO

ANNOTATE

Analyze Text Structure

An author may include an **anecdote**, or brief story, within the story to illustrate an important point or theme in the text. Read paragraphs 1–11 to learn about an event that took place much earlier than the other events described in the text.

Underline evidence that tells you how the author is using chronological text structure to put this anecdote into context for the reader.

1 ZENI WATCHED THE WOODEN BAT THWACK THE BASEBALL, hurling it high and straight. He was eight years old, and it was the first time he'd seen a baseball game, but he was hooked.

2 "Father, I want to play!" he told his dad.

3 "You're too small," his father said.

4 "Too frail," added his mother.

5 But Zeni didn't listen. He had to play.

6 The other kids laughed at him.

7 "Zeni, you're a mouse!" one boy hooted.

8 "A teeny tiny one!" another kid called.

9 None of it mattered. When Zeni had a ball or bat in his hand, he felt like a giant. And soon he played like one.

10 Many springs had passed since that first game, years of playing in the chill of winter and the sweat of summer. Zeni got taller and stronger and better at baseball.

11 "Why are you wasting time with a silly game?" his mother asked.

12 "You should study and become a doctor," his father said. "Or a lawyer."

13 But Zeni knew exactly what he wanted to do, and when he grew up, he coached, managed, and played baseball in the Fresno Nisei League and the Fresno Twilight League. He was barely five feet tall and weighed only one hundred pounds, but he was a star player, casting a big shadow in baseball.

14   Zeni was chosen to play with star members of the New York Yankees. He led his teams in exhibition games in Japan. He even arranged for Babe Ruth to play there. But that world collapsed for him when the Japanese attacked Pearl Harbor in 1941. For the first time since he had picked up a bat, Zeni felt as if he didn't measure up.

15   The United States was at war with Japan, and 120,000 Americans of Japanese descent who lived on the West Coast were forced into ten internment camps, most in the desert. The government considered these Japanese Americans to be possible spies and, without evidence or trials, locked them up—men, women, and children. American citizens, all were treated like prisoners of war, housed in barracks and penned in with barbed wire.

CLOSE READ

Summarize a Text

Highlight information that you would include in a summary of these paragraphs.

descent the family background or national origin of a person

internment related to confinement, as if in a prison, often during a war

16 **ZENI, HIS WIFE, AND THEIR TWO TEENAGE SONS WERE SENT** to a camp in Gila River, Arizona. Outside, the camp was bleak and gray and dusty. Inside, the barracks were stark, with crowded rows of cots and not much else. Families bustled around, trying to make a home out of nothing, hanging up curtains, arranging tea sets on footlockers, piling dolls and stuffed animals on cots.

17 Zeni stood staring at the dry earth, which was broken up every now and then by a few scrubby bits of green. In all the brown and gray, with dull, coppery sky overhead, he felt as if he were shrinking into a tiny hard ball.

18 There was only one thing that could make the desert camp a home—baseball. Zeni unpacked his favorite photo, the one that showed him in uniform, lined up with baseball legends Babe Ruth and Lou Gehrig towering like redwood trees beside him. He had played with the Yankee stars in an exhibition game back home in Fresno, and he hadn't felt small at all. He pinned the picture up over his bed. He was going to play baseball again. Here, in the desolate middle of nowhere.

Analyze Text Structure

Underline details that show plot events unfolding in time order.

desolate empty, lonely, and unhappy

CLOSE READ

Summarize a Text

Highlight information that you should include in a summary of how Zeni built his baseball field.

19   First he would need a playing field. There was plenty of empty space, but it was dotted with sagebrush and clotted with rocks. It didn't look like much of a field.

20   Zeni started by chopping down the plants and digging up the rocks, spending long hours in the blazing sun.

21   "What are you doing, Dad?" his son Howard asked.

22   "Can't play baseball without a field," Zeni grunted.

23   "We're going to play baseball?" Howard grinned and started picking up rocks, too.

24   Soon Howard's brother, Harvey, joined them. Then other boys and men drifted to where Zeni and his sons were bent over in the glaring heat. By the end of the day, dozens of people were working on the field, not planting a crop but unplanting, making the ground a smooth surface.

25   Once the brush and the biggest rocks had been cleared, Howard and Harvey were ready to set up the bases. "Looks good," Howard said. "We're almost set."

26   Zeni shook his head. "Nowhere close. We're making a real ballpark, and we'll do it right." He walked over to the camp commander's office. Ten minutes later, he emerged into the bright sun, smiling.

27   "We've got it!" He clapped his hands.

28   "What?" asked Howard. "What have we got?"

29   "A bulldozer to level the field," Zeni replied. "The commander said we can borrow the camp's."

30   As Zeni drove the bulldozer, crowds gathered to watch.

31   "What's he doing?" an old woman asked her grandson.

32   "He's making a baseball field," the young man answered.

33   "A baseball field? Whatever for?" she asked.

34   Her son smiled. "So we can play."

35   Once the ground had been smoothed, Harvey brought out his bat and ball. "Now we can play, right?" he asked.

36   Zeni shook his head. He still wasn't satisfied. The wind kicked up so much dust from the dry soil that the players would be eating dirt.

37   "We have to do this right." He looked around the camp, hoping to find something to solve the dust problem. Then he got an idea. He diverted an irrigation line to the field and flooded it with water. Once the heat had dried the ground, the dirt was baked into clay—a clean, hard surface without all the dust.

38   "Now, Dad?" asked Howard, tossing a ball between his hands. "It looks great!"

39   "Almost," Zeni answered. "But we're not there yet."

CLOSE READ

Analyze Text Structure

<u>Underline</u> evidence about a problem and a solution.

diverted changed the direction of

167

Analyze Text Structure

Underline details that show how events are described in chronological order.

spectators people who watch an event

40   The irrigation line gave Zeni another idea. He laid pipe from the laundry room to the field and planted grass in the infield and quick-growing castor beans along the edge of the outfield. The pipe fed water to the plants, and soon the clay and grass took on the shape of a baseball field with a castor bean fence. Zeni smiled. Now it was beginning to look real.

41   "Come on, Dad," Howard urged. "Can't we at least mark the bases now?"

42   "Go ahead," Zeni agreed. "But we're not done yet."

43   Howard used flour to chalk the foul lines, and his mom sewed the bases from rice sacks.

44   "It's perfect!" Harvey said.

45   "What about the spectators, the fans?" Zeni asked. "Where will they go?"

46   Both boys shrugged. "Can't they just stand around?" Howard asked.

47   "Or we can build rows of bleachers," Zeni said. "Like on a real baseball field."

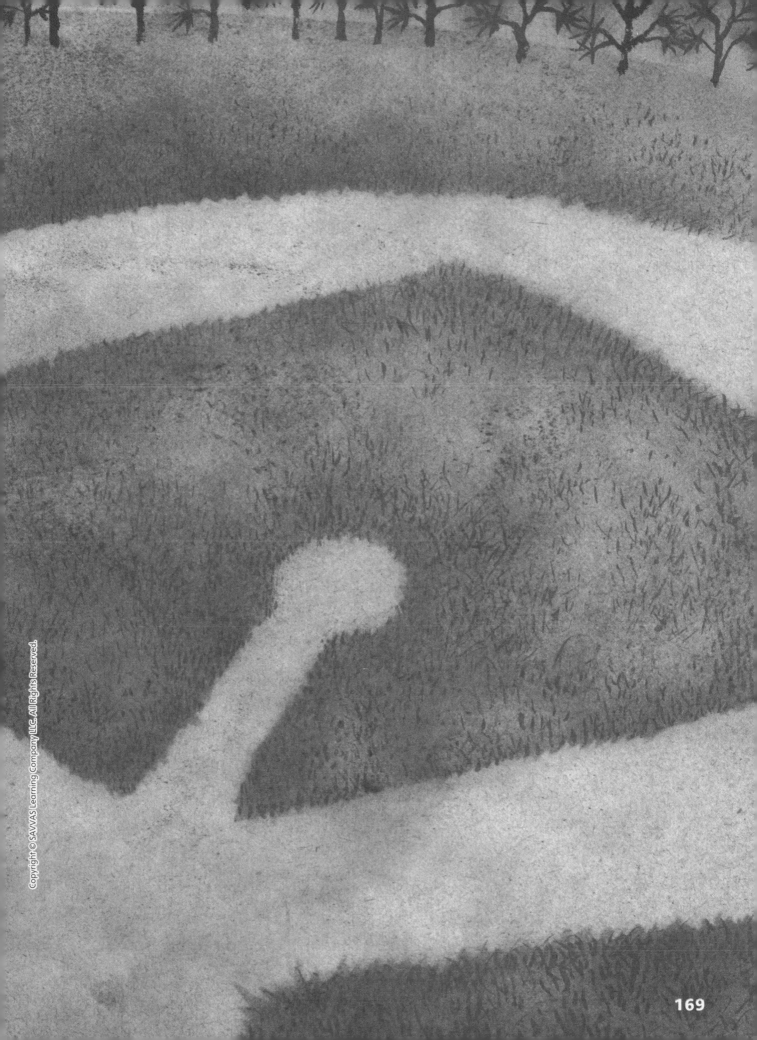

170

48   That night Zeni and his sons snuck out of their barracks. They were not allowed outside after dark. Zeni felt like a boy again, tiptoeing out of the house with his bat and glove so his parents wouldn't see him.

49   A guard's light swept across the yard, and Zeni motioned to the boys to flatten themselves against the barracks. They waited for the beam to pass, then crept on. They didn't know that the guard had seen them but the commander had told him to let them go, so long as they didn't escape. The commander was curious to see what Zeni wanted now.

50   The three of them scrounged wood from the fence surrounding the camp. They removed every other post, careful not to damage the fencing. Then they took wood from the camp lumberyard. That gave them enough material to build a backstop and five rows of bleachers behind it.

CLOSE READ

Vocabulary in Context

Determine the meaning of *scrounged* in paragraph 50.

Underline context clues that support your definition.

Summarize a Text

Highlight information that you would use to retell what happened after the bleachers were completed.

51   The next day they set to work again, this time sawing wood and nailing boards. When Howard finished hammering the last row of seats, he wiped the sweat from his forehead and gaped at what they had made. There, in the middle of the desert, on the edge of an internment camp, was an official-looking baseball field. The rest of the place slumped, dreary and sad, but the baseball field glowed green with hope.

52   "Now, Dad?" Harvey asked.

53   "Almost." Zeni smiled. "We have the field. Now we need the equipment."

54   He passed a hat among the families, collecting money for gear. In an hour he had enough to send for bats, balls, mitts, and hats from Holman's Sporting Goods back home in Fresno. Several women sewed uniforms out of potato sacks.

55   When the box of equipment arrived, Zeni let Howard open it. "Now, Howard," he said. "Now we can play ball!"

56 **THAT FIRST GAME ON A BRIGHT MAY DAY, HALF THE** camp turned out to watch the teams that Zeni had organized. A breeze stirred the new grass. The sun bathed everything in a gentle warmth. It was a perfect day for a baseball game. Six thousand people filled the bleachers and spilled onto the scrubby ground behind them and along the sides of the stands.

57 Zeni leaned over home plate, the bat held firmly in his hands. He looked at Howard, already on first base; at Harvey, now on second; at the neat white lines marking the field. His eyes scanned the bleachers filled with cheering fans. He watched the pitcher cradling the ball, pulling back his arm, getting ready to throw.

58 Zeni focused on the blur of white as it zoomed closer. The weight of the bat felt so familiar and natural, it was like a part of his body. He waited until just the right moment . . .

CLOSE READ

Analyze Text Structure

<u>Underline</u> text evidence that helps you understand the organization of the biography by describing Zeni's experiences in time order.

59   *Whack.* The bat met the ball with a crisp, splintering sound. Zeni threw the bat down and ran. He ran to first base, then second, then third, his eyes following the arc of the ball as it soared up and away, far over the barbed wire fence.

Analyze Text Structure

Underline details that show the order of events.

60   Howard and Harvey jogged to home plate before him, arms raised, grins plastered on their faces. "Now!" they yelled. "Now!"

61   "Now!" Zeni shouted back. He knew he was still behind a barbed wire fence, but he felt completely free, as airy and light as the ball he had sent flying.

Summarize a Text

Highlight details that you would use to paraphrase what baseball meant to Zeni.

62   Right now there was nothing else he wanted to do. Just this, right now, right here. It didn't matter whether his team won or lost. Like the powerful champion he was, he felt he could touch the sky if he wanted. "Now!" he roared as he crossed home plate.

63   He felt ten feet tall, playing the game he loved so much. Nothing would ever make him feel small again.

Develop Vocabulary

In narrative nonfiction, authors often describe events using domain-specific words, or words that are specific to the topic. These words help the reader determine the relationship between the events and people in the text.

My TURN Write the meaning of each word. Then use each word in a sentence that explains how the Japanese attack on Pearl Harbor affected Zeni's life.

Word	Definition	Sentence Related to Zeni's Life
descent		
internment		
spectators		

Check for Understanding

My TURN Look back at the text to answer the questions.

1. What characteristics tell you that *Barbed Wire Baseball* is a biography?

2. Why does Marissa Moss include dialogue in a biography?

3. Why did other people from the internment camp help Zeni make a baseball field?

4. Analyze the way Zeni approached his baseball field project. What does that tell you about him?

Analyze Text Structure

Biographies often use **chronological**, or time order, **text structure** to organize ideas. When an author's purpose is to inform the reader about a real person, chronological order can help the reader understand important events and how they affect the life of the person in the biography.

1. **My TURN** Go to the Close Read notes in *Barbed Wire Baseball* and underline evidence that reveals text structure.

2. **Text Evidence** Use the parts you underlined to complete the chart and explain how the text structure reveals author's purpose.

Event 1:

What I Learned About Zeni:

Event 2:

What I Learned About Zeni:

Event 3:

What I Learned About Zeni:

How Text Structure Reveals Author's Purpose:

Summarize a Text

Use chronological text structure to **summarize**. In a summary of a biography, include only the most important events and details.

1. **My TURN** Go back to the Close Read notes and highlight parts of the text to include in a summary.

2. **Text Evidence** Use your highlighted text to complete the chart. Identify the signal words that Marissa Moss uses to create a chronological text structure.

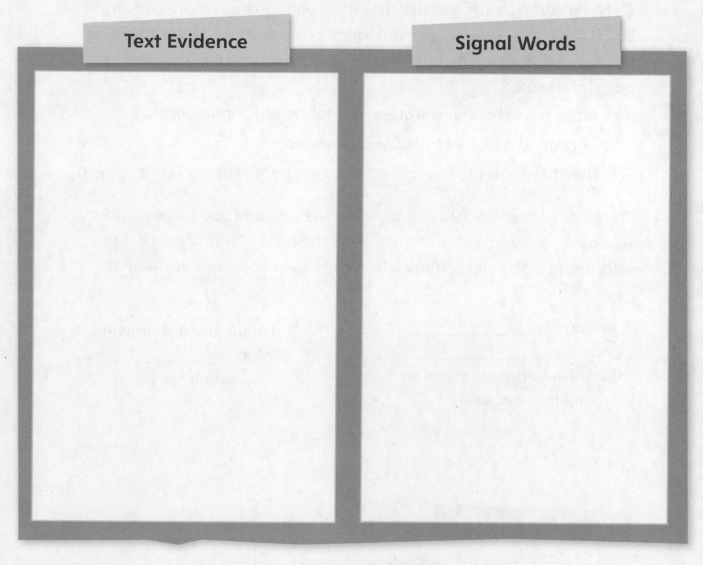

Text Evidence	Signal Words

On a separate sheet of paper, use your text evidence to summarize the text. Include similar signal words to retell events in order.

Reflect and Share

Talk About It In *Barbed Wire Baseball*, Zeni uses the resources around him in the internment camp to build a baseball field. What other uses of resources have you read about this week? Were these examples as creative or inventive as Zeni's? Discuss specific ideas in the texts to support your opinion.

Cite Accurate Information Make your opinion more convincing by discussing specific, important ideas in the texts and by supporting the ideas with accurate information. Before you begin your discussion, gather information.

- Write a brief opinion statement that begins, *I think that* . . .
- Choose two or three texts you have read.
- Use sticky notes to mark lines telling ideas that support your opinion.

To cite accurately, quote directly from the text and use page numbers. By doing this, you give other students the ability to verify your information. Use the sentence frames to help you cite information:

In the text _____, I read about _____. This information supports my opinion because . . .

I understand your point, but in _____ the author says . . .

Weekly Question

How can people influence the places where they live?

Academic Vocabulary

Learning Goal

I can develop knowledge about language to make connections between reading and writing.

Parts of speech are word categories that include:

- **nouns,** or words that name people, places, or things

- **verbs,** or words that tell an action or state of being

- **adjectives,** or words describing the people, places, or things that nouns name

- **adverbs,** or words that tell how, when, or where something happens

Many words can be used as more than one part of speech.

My TURN For each sentence,

1. **Underline** the form of the academic vocabulary word in the sentence.

2. **Identify** the word's part of speech.

3. **Write** your own sentence using the same word but as a different part of speech.

Sentence	Part of Speech	My Sentence
He <u>habitually</u> came to class prepared.	adverb	He made it a habit to always be early. (noun)
The leader made a contribution to help her community.		
One of the significant parts of the mission is to help young people.		
The reporter exposed the story quickly.		

Prefixes *mis-, en-, em-*

Prefixes are word parts that are added to the beginning of main, or base, words. The prefix *mis-* means "not" or "the opposite of." The prefixes *en-* and *em-* can mean "in," "provide with," or "cause to be." Prefixes change the meaning of base words.

When you read words with the prefixes *mis-, en-,* or *-em,* the main, or base words, are read the same. For example, in the word *mislead,* the base word *lead* is read the same with or without the prefix.

My TURN Read the following words with prefixes. Then write the meaning of each word.

1. empower _____

_____

2. misspell _____

_____

3. enlarge _____

_____

4. misplace _____

_____

5. endanger _____

_____

6. misbehave _____

_____

Read Like a Writer

An **author's purpose** is the reason why an author writes a text, such as to inform, persuade, entertain, or express ideas and feelings. Analyze details to determine and explain the author's purpose.

Model ! Read the text from *Barbed Wire Baseball*.

> Zeni was chosen to play with star members of the New York Yankees.

1. **Identify** Marissa Moss gives details about Zeni's baseball career.

2. **Question** How does this detail reveal the author's purpose?

3. **Conclude** The detail gives information about an important part of Zeni's life. It reveals that the author's main purpose is to inform.

Read the text.

> He had played with the Yankee stars in an exhibition game back home in Fresno, and he hadn't felt small at all.

My TURN Follow the steps to explain the author's purpose.

1. **Identify** This passage describes _____

_____

2. **Question** How does this detail support the author's purpose?

3. **Conclude** This detail _____

_____

_____

Write for a Reader

Authors include specific facts and details to support their purpose for writing and reveal their overall message.

What information do you want readers to know after reading your writing?

My TURN Marissa Moss included facts and details in *Barbed Wire Baseball* to inform readers about how historical events shaped Zeni's life. Now analyze an important event that affected your life. What details would you include to reveal your purpose for writing and your overall message?

1. Choose an important event in your life that you would like to write about. What would your purpose be for writing about it? What facts and details could you include to support that purpose?

   Purpose: _____

   Facts and Details: _____

   _____

   _____

   _____

2. Write a passage about the event you chose. Include the facts and details that support your purpose for writing and reveal your message.

   _____

   _____

   _____

   _____

   _____

   _____

   _____

Spell Words with Prefixes

The **prefixes *mis-*, *en-*, and *em-*** are word parts that are added before a base word. These prefixes do not change the spelling of the base word.

My TURN Read the words. Sort and spell the words under the appropriate prefix.

SPELLING WORDS

misspell	misbehave	misplace	enlarge
enable	enclosed	empower	encourage
misquote	mishandle	encode	enlighten
engulf	enclosure	endangered	misjudge
misfortune	misadventure	misunderstand	embed

mis-

_____

_____

_____

_____

_____

_____

_____

en-

_____

_____

_____

_____

_____

_____

_____

em-

_____

_____

_____

_____

_____

_____

_____

Fix Sentence Fragments

A sentence has a subject and a predicate, which together form a complete thought. In a **sentence fragment**, either the subject or the predicate is missing. To fix a sentence fragment, add the missing part or connect it to the sentence that precedes it.

Fragment	How to Fix It	Corrected Sentence
Was chosen to play with stars of the New York Yankees.	add a subject	<u>Zeni</u> was chosen to play with stars of the New York Yankees.
Zeni, his wife, and their two teenage sons.	add a predicate	Zeni, his wife, and their two teenage sons <u>were sent to a camp in Gila River, Arizona.</u>
Crowds gathered to watch Zeni. As he drove the bulldozer.	connect to preceding sentence	Crowds gathered to watch Zeni <u>as he drove the bulldozer.</u>

My TURN Fix the sentence fragments in the draft. Remember to change capital letters to lowercase letters when joining fragments to preceding sentences.

> Zeni became a famous baseball player. Even though he was
>
> not very tall or very big. Treated him like a prisoner of war.
>
> Zeni made a baseball field. In the internment camp. Zeni could
>
> play baseball. After the bleachers were built. He felt free. Even
>
> though he was behind barbed wire.

Edit for Irregular Verbs

For regular verbs, you add -ed to show past tense. The -ed form is also used with *have*, *has*, and *had* for regular verbs.

Regular	walk	walked	have walked
	fix	fixed	has fixed
	blend	blended	had blended

Irregular verbs have different forms for the past and with the helping verbs *has*, *had*, or *have*. Because each irregular verb is different, writers have to learn the forms and how to spell them or they have to look them up in a dictionary.

Irregular	think	thought	have thought
	go	went	has gone
	see	saw	had seen

My TURN Complete the blanks with past tense irregular verbs that make sense in the passage.

Janice _____ she asked to be on my swim team this summer. Janice is a super tennis player. So I _____ Janice a letter in which I _____ her I _____ she would be a great addition to the tennis team instead.

My TURN Edit one of your drafts so that all irregular verbs are used and spelled correctly.

Edit for Punctuation Marks

Combine short sentences when the ideas go together. This creates a **compound sentence**. To write a compound sentence, use a comma and a conjunction (such as *and, so,* or *but*).

Sentence 1	Comma and Conjunction	Sentence 2
I sat at the table	, but	I wanted to get up right away.
You scared the cat	, and	now it will hide all afternoon.

Use **apostrophes** to create the possessive forms of nouns. For example, the possessive of *horse* is *horse's*, and the possessive of *Juan* is *Juan's*.

Use **quotation marks** to correctly punctuate dialogue in a personal narrative. For example, correctly punctuated dialogue might look like this: Jessica turned to her friend and asked, "Do you want to play a game?"

My TURN Edit the following paragraph to ensure correct punctuation.

Let's go to the playground, I said to Leanna. She smiled and I grabbed the bag of soccer balls. We have time to practice before the game, I added, returning Leannas smile.

In a personal narrative, the writer's own thoughts may be written and punctuated as dialogue.

My TURN Edit one of your own drafts to check that you have used punctuation marks correctly.

Publish and Celebrate

Once your personal narrative is finished, it is time to publish it for an audience. Consider the audience—classmates, younger readers, adults. Then publish it in a school or local paper, on a bulletin board, or wherever your audience might read it.

My TURN Complete these sentences to reflect on your writing experience. Use cursive writing.

I decided to publish my personal narrative in or on

_____

_____

_____

I told readers about the narrator of my personal narrative by

_____

_____

_____

The concrete words, adjectives, and adverbs I used in my personal narrative helped make it

_____

_____

_____

The next time I publish a personal narrative, I want to

_____

_____

_____

_____

Prepare for Assessment

My TURN   Follow a plan as you prepare to write a personal narrative in response to a prompt.

1. **Study the prompt.**

   You will receive an assignment called a writing prompt. Read the prompt carefully. Highlight the type of writing you must do. <u>Underline</u> the topic you are supposed to write about.

   > **Prompt:** Write a personal narrative about your first experience in a new place.

2. **Brainstorm.**

   > List three personal experiences you could write about. Then highlight your favorite.

3. **Organize and plan your personal narrative.**

   > Introduction → Event 1 → Next Events → Turning Point → Final Event → Conclusion

4. **Write your draft.**

   > Remember to orient readers through your introduction and wrap up the narrator's experience in your conclusion.

   Remember, a great personal narrative develops an engaging idea.

5. **Revise and edit your personal narrative.**

   > Apply the skills and rules you have learned to polish your writing and correct mistakes.

Assessment

My TURN Before you write a personal narrative for your assessment, rate how well you understand the skills you have learned in this unit. Go back and review any skills you mark "No."

		Yes!	No
Ideas and Organization	◐ I can brainstorm an engaging idea.	❑	❑
	◐ I can introduce people and a situation.	❑	❑
	◐ I can describe a setting and organize events.	❑	❑
	◐ I can end the narrative with a conclusion.	❑	❑
Craft	◐ I can include relevant details.	❑	❑
	◐ I can use concrete words and phrases.	❑	❑
	◐ I can include sensory details.	❑	❑
	◐ I can write dialogue between people.	❑	❑
	◐ I can use transition words and phrases.	❑	❑
	◐ I can add and delete ideas for clarity.	❑	❑
Conventions	◐ I can use adjectives and adverbs correctly.	❑	❑
	◐ I can use reflexive and relative pronouns.	❑	❑
	◐ I can recognize and use irregular verbs.	❑	❑
	◐ I can edit compound sentences for commas and dialogue for quotation marks.	❑	❑

Networks

UNIT THEME

TURN and TALK Connect to Theme

In this unit, you learned many new words to talk about *Networks*. With a partner, choose an academic vocabulary word for each selection. Find a quotation from each selection that best illustrates the word. Explain why that word fits that quotation.

WEEK 3

"Twins in Space"

_____

_____

_____

_____

_____

_____

BOOK CLUB

WEEK 2

Rare Treasure: Mary Anning and Her Remarkable Discoveries

_____

_____

_____

_____

BOOK CLUB

WEEK 1

Reaching for the Moon

_____

_____

_____

198

WEEK 4

Life at the Top

_____

_____

_____

_____

Life at the Top
by Veronica Ellis

WEEK 6

Barbed Wire BASEBALL
by Marissa Moss

BOOK CLUB

WEEK 5

Barbed Wire Baseball

_____

_____

_____

_____

Essential Question

My TURN

In your notebook, answer the Essential Question: How can a place affect how we live?

BOOK CLUB

Project

WEEK 6

Now it is time to apply what you learned about *Networks* in your **WEEK 6 PROJECT**: Make It a Landmark!

Make It a Landmark!

Activity

Think of a place in your community that you believe should be made a historical landmark to save or preserve it for future generations. Create a brochure to tell your audience about this place and convince them that it ought to be a landmark.

RESEARCH

Research Articles

With your partner, read "Historic Landmarks" to generate questions. Then make a research plan for creating your brochure by listing the steps needed. Follow your plan. Ask your teacher for help if necessary.

1 Historic Landmarks

2 Save Our Theater

3 Ellis Island: Gateway to America

Generate Questions

COLLABORATE After reading "Historic Landmarks," generate three questions about landmarks. List your questions here.

1. _____

2. _____

3. _____

Use Academic Words

COLLABORATE In this unit, you learned many words related to the theme, *Networks*. Work collaboratively with your partner to add more academic vocabulary words to each category. If appropriate, use this vocabulary when you write your brochure.

Academic Vocabulary	Word Forms	Synonyms	Antonyms
contribute	contributes contributed contribution	give provide donate	refuse destroy withdraw
exposed	expose exposing unexposed	open unguarded vulnerable	protected closed defended
habit	habits habitual habit-forming	routine custom pattern	irregularity occasional infrequent
severe	severity severest severely	strict harsh rigid	mild kind undemanding
significant	significance insignificant significantly	important noteworthy meaningful	trivial unimportant minor

A Matter of Opinion

A **claim** is an opinion. **Evidence** is information I get from my reading about the topic that helps support my claim.

In argumentative writing, the author gives an opinion about a topic. Usually the author tries to convince the reader that his or her opinion is correct. When reading opinion essays, look for

- a claim, or opinion,
- one or more reasons that support the claim, and
- facts and other evidence that support your reasons.

RESEARCH

COLLABORATE With your partner, read the Research Article "Save Our Theater." Then answer the following questions about the article and the author's claims and evidence.

1. What is the writer's claim, or opinion?

2. Who in town might be opposed to saving the theater? Why?

3. Which facts and details support the author's claim?

Plan Your Research

COLLABORATE Before you begin researching landmarks, you will need to come up with a research plan. Use the activity below to help you write a claim and plan how you will look for evidence.

Definition	Examples
CLAIMS A claim is a statement that tries to persuade or convince a reader to agree with an opinion. A claim • defines your goal, • is specific, and • is supported with evidence. Read the two examples in the right column. This writer is writing an argumentative brochure about playgrounds. Then, with your partner, write a claim for which place should become a historical landmark.	Playgrounds Claim • I like Bartlett Playground best. No • Bartlett Playground offers the best park experience in our community. Yes! My claim: _____ _____ _____
EVIDENCE You can support your claim with evidence, such as • facts • statistics • examples • quotations	**Fact:** Adams Playground has not been renovated since 2002. **Statistic:** The community raised $25,000 to improve Bartlett Playground. **Example:** Bartlett Playground added new equipment, such as a new climbing structure. **Quote:** "Lots of parents stop by my office to complain," said Roberta Han, the city's mayor.

With your partner, list some possible options for finding evidence for your landmark research project.

HiT the STREETS!

Field research involves going to visit a place you are writing about so you can learn as much as possible about it. Field research may involve drawing or photographing the place or writing a careful description. Your own experiences can be important parts of your research.

Keep in mind your audience and what your audience will likely know or not know about your place. Describing a place in detail can help your audience understand and appreciate the place.

EXAMPLE For their argumentative brochure, Samuel and Livia have been asked to find the best playground in their community. With a trusted adult, they do field research by visiting several playgrounds. They take pictures and note such information as the number and condition of each piece of play equipment, the surface under the equipment, the amount of play space, and so on. They can use this information to help them decide which playground is the best and convince others that they are right.

Adams Playground has broken glass.

Bartlett Playground has a great climbing structure.

Carter Playground has few pieces of play equipment.

Their field research suggests that Bartlett Playground is the best playground of the three.

COLLABORATE Note how field research helped Samuel and Livia learn about the playgrounds. Now, do field research with your partner and an adult to learn about your landmark. If you are not able to visit your landmark in person, work with your partner to visualize your chosen landmark.

Then fill in the graphic organizer below. Include important details and information about your landmark. Draw a picture of the place in the top box. Include a description and any special features.

Illustration:

General Description:

Special Features:

*

*

*

Review the information you have. What other information about the place do you need to find?

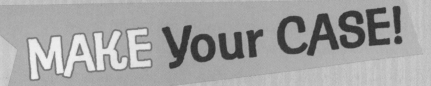

Writers use **argumentative texts** to convince people that their opinions are valid. They make claims, give reasons, and support those reasons with evidence.

Creating a brochure is one way of presenting an argumentative text. Look through brochures in your classroom and at home. Pay attention to how they look and how they share information through visuals and text. When you create a brochure, you will

- use one sheet of paper folded into thirds to make six sections.
- use texts and illustrations to make and support your claims.
- put a different reason and its evidence on each section of the brochure.

COLLABORATE Read the Student Model. Talk with your partner about how to create a brochure that presents an argumentative text.

Now You Try It!

Discuss the checklist with your partner. Work together to follow the steps as you create your persuasive brochure.

Make sure your brochure

☐ consists of six sections.

☐ includes both art and text.

☐ states a specific claim.

☐ provides evidence and reasons to support your claim.

Student Model

Front

Middle Panel | Back Panel | Cover Panel

Adams Playground is not in very good shape. It has good play equipment. It is filled with litter and broken glass. It needs a good cleanup before it will be a good place for kids to spend time!

There are 3 playgrounds in our community: Adams, Bartlett, and Carter.

Which Is the BEST PLAYGROUND in Our Community?

By Samuel and Livia

Back, inside of brochure

Bartlett Playground has some great new play equipment, such as a climbing structure that kids really seem to love. The playground is clean. The playground is big. The playground is safe.

Carter Playground is very clean, and it has enough space for lots of kids to play at the same time. What it doesn't have is up-to-date equipment. Kids might become bored quickly.

Underline the claim.

You should go to **Bartlett Playground**. It is truly the best in our community!

Highlight a reason and a fact that supports it. Tell your partner how the fact supports the claim.

Go to the Source

When you do research, you use sources to find information. Sources can be books, articles, online resources, or even other people. **Primary** sources are written or made by people who have firsthand knowledge of an event or topic. **Secondary** sources are created by people who did not participate in an event. People create secondary sources by using information from primary sources.

Primary Sources	Secondary Sources
• firsthand account of an event • interview • photographs from the event • original government document • diary or journal entry	• textbook • biography • encyclopedia entry
Example of a primary source: A diary entry written by a baseball player after winning the World Series. The baseball player writes what he experienced and how he felt when the team won.	**Example of a secondary source:** An article written by someone who did not directly experience the World Series game. The person did research about the game by watching interviews with the winning team and reading articles written by journalists who were present at the game.

📖 **RESEARCH**

COLLABORATE Read the Research Article "Ellis Island: Gateway to America." Is the article a primary source or a secondary source? Use what you know about sources to identify at least one primary source and one secondary source for your research on creating a historical landmark.

COLLABORATE Read the article excerpt. Answer the questions.

Carter Playground on Elm Street is one of the least popular playgrounds in the city. It is also one of the most deserted. On a typical Saturday afternoon not long ago, just three children were playing on the equipment.

"It's not a very nice playground," says Adam Peters, 10. "The slides are old and the swings are in bad shape." He says he plays at Carter only because the other playgrounds in town are too far away to walk to.

Susan Nimms, 43, lives across the street from the playground. She agrees with Adam. "I hardly ever see children playing at Carter," she says. "Even on a beautiful sunny day almost no one is there. It's a shame!"

The city's mayor, Roberta Han, has never visited Carter but admits that there may be a problem. "Lots of parents stop by my office to complain," she says. "I wish we had the money to fix things!"

1. Is Adam Peters a primary source or secondary source? Explain.

_____

_____

2. Is Susan Nimms a primary source or secondary source? Explain.

_____

_____

3. Is Roberta Han a primary source or secondary source? Explain.

_____

_____

Incorporate MEDiA

Brochures need plenty of images. Samuel and Livia used photographs. You can also use maps, diagrams, graphs, charts, or other visuals that will support your claim and interest your audience. Using visuals will show your understanding of the information.

A **map** shows where people can find the landmark in your community.

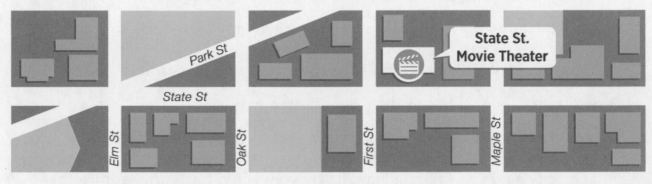

A **diagram** shows interesting features of the landmark.

A **graph** or **chart** can show evidence to support your claims.

COLLABORATE With your partner, brainstorm how you could use each of the following types of media in your project. On the note cards, write *what* information you would show and *where* in your brochure it would work best. If you have the opportunity, go online to find some examples.

Drawings or Photographs	Maps
What?	What?
Where?	Where?

Diagrams	Graphs or Charts
What?	What?
Where?	Where?

Revise

Revise Sentence Structure Reread your brochure with your partner. Have you

- ☐ varied sentence types and lengths?
- ☐ varied sentence beginnings?
- ☐ added to or combined sentences to connect and clarify ideas?
- ☐ deleted or combined sentences to express ideas precisely?

Revise Sentences

The writers of the brochure about playgrounds reread their work. They saw that some of their sentences were too much alike. They made the following revisions to vary their sentences to connect or emphasize important ideas and make their writing more interesting.

Bartlett Playground has some great new play equipment, such as a climbing structure that kids really seem to love. The playground is clean. ~~The playground is big. The~~ ^and^ Just as important, the playground is safe.

Edit

Conventions Read your text again. Check that you used the following conventions correctly:

- ☐ descriptive adjectives
- ☐ comparative adjectives (*bigger*, *older*)
- ☐ superlative adjectives (*biggest*, *oldest*)

Peer Review

COLLABORATE Exchange brochures with another pair. As you read the other pair's brochure, identify the claim, reasons, and supporting evidence. In addition, ask yourself how the brochure looks and how the authors used images to emphasize important ideas and engage their audience. Finally, try to identify which of the sources they used are primary sources and which are secondary sources.

Time to Celebrate!

COLLABORATE As a class, create a brochure rack so you can share your brochures with other groups or classes. Then orally present your brochure to another group. Be sure to make eye contact as you present, and speak clearly and at a natural rate and volume. How did the other group react? What did they like about your presentation? What suggestions or changes did they have? Write their reactions here. Finally, have groups vote on the most convincing brochure.

_____

_____

_____

_____

Reflect on Your Project

My TURN Think about your brochure. Which parts do you think are strongest? Which parts need improvement? Write your thoughts here.

Strengths

_____

_____

Areas of Improvement

_____

_____

_____

Reflect on Your Goals

Look back at your unit goals.
Use a different color to rate yourself again.

Reflect on Your Reading

When you read fiction, it is important to think about how you would react or how you would feel if you were one of the characters.

Share a personal connection you made while reading one of your independent reading texts. Describe how a scene or section reminded you of when something similar happened to you.

_____

_____

_____

_____

_____

Reflect on Your Writing

How did your writing improve during this unit? Explain.

_____

_____

_____

_____

_____

Adaptations

Essential Question

How do living things adapt to the world around them?

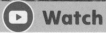 **Watch**

"Adapt to Survive"

TURN and TALK

What does it mean for living things to adapt, or change?

SAVVAS
realize™
Go ONLINE for
all lessons.

- VIDEO
- AUDIO
- INTERACTIVITY
- GAME
- ANNOTATE
- BOOK
- RESEARCH

Spotlight on Informational Text

READING WORKSHOP

Infographic: Why Animals Adapt

Feathers: Not Just for Flying .... Informational Text
by Melissa Stewart

Media: Survival Adaptations

Animal Mimics .... Informational Text
by Marie Racanelli

Primary Source: Saving Elephants

from ***Minn of the Mississippi*** .... Fiction
by Holling Clancy Holling

Infographic: Part of a Habitat

from ***Butterfly Eyes and Other Secrets of the Meadow*** .... Poetry
by Joyce Sidman

Infographic: Many Ways to Be One of a Kind

The Weird and Wonderful Echidna and ***The Very Peculiar Platypus*** .... Informational Texts
by Mike Jung | by Wade Hudson

READING-WRITING BRIDGE

• Academic Vocabulary • Word Study
• **Read Like a Writer** • **Write for a Reader**
• Spelling • Language and Conventions

WRITING WORKSHOP

• Introduce and Immerse • Develop Elements   **Informational Text**
• Develop Structure • Writer's Craft
• Publish, Celebrate, and Assess

PROJECT-BASED INQUIRY

• Inquire • Research • Collaborate

UNIT
2

Independent Reading

Establishing a purpose for reading is a good way to help you select a text that you will enjoy. Setting a goal for your reading can help you grow as a reader.

- -

Step 1 Decide your purpose for reading. Ask yourself:

What is my purpose for reading?

○ Am I reading for enjoyment?

○ Am I reading to find out about a topic?

○ Do I want to read more by an author?

- -

Step 2 Set a goal for your independent reading. Here are some examples. You can choose one of these or create your own.

- I want to read nonfiction similar to a book I have already read.
- I want to try a different genre, such as *historical fiction*.
- I want to read a more challenging book.
- I want to read for a sustained period of time.

My goal for independent reading is

_____

_____

Practice setting a purpose and goal for reading as you select the text you will read.

Independent Reading Log

Date	Book	Genre	Pages Read	Minutes Read	My Ratings
					☆☆☆☆☆

Unit Goals

Shade in the circle to rate how well you meet each goal now.

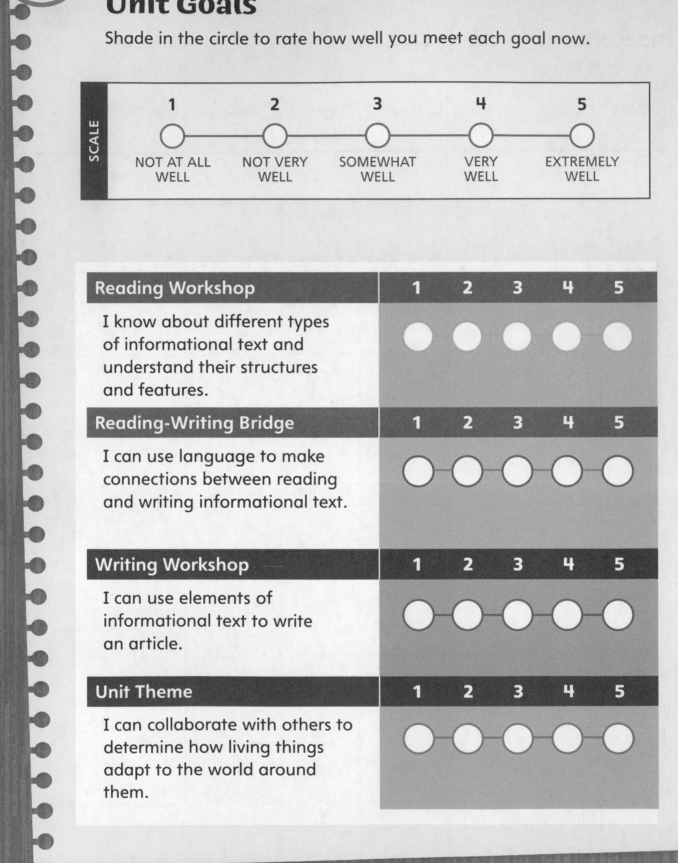

SCALE

1	2	3	4	5
NOT AT ALL WELL	NOT VERY WELL	SOMEWHAT WELL	VERY WELL	EXTREMELY WELL

Reading Workshop

I know about different types of informational text and understand their structures and features.

| 1 | 2 | 3 | 4 | 5 |

Reading-Writing Bridge

I can use language to make connections between reading and writing informational text.

| 1 | 2 | 3 | 4 | 5 |

Writing Workshop

I can use elements of informational text to write an article.

| 1 | 2 | 3 | 4 | 5 |

Unit Theme

I can collaborate with others to determine how living things adapt to the world around them.

| 1 | 2 | 3 | 4 | 5 |

Academic Vocabulary

Use these words to talk about this unit's theme, *Adaptations*: *acquire*, *classified*, *defense*, *sufficient*, and *survive*.

My TURN Use the definitions to make connections between the newly acquired vocabulary words.

Academic Vocabulary	Definition
acquire	get; take; obtain
classified	categorized; grouped with
defense	someone or something that protects
sufficient	enough for a particular purpose
survive	stay alive; live through a dangerous event

1. How are the words *defense* and *acquire* similar, and how are they different?

_____

_____

_____

_____

2. What things should a person have a *sufficient* amount of to *survive*?

_____

_____

_____

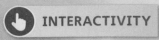
INTERACTIVITY

Why ANIMALS ADAPT

ADAPTATIONS

Behaviors or physical features, called adaptations, help living things survive in their environment.

BEHAVIORAL ADAPTATIONS
Many bird species migrate to warmer weather as winter approaches.

PHYSICAL ADAPTATIONS
The Arctic fox has a thick, white winter coat that keeps the animal warm and allows it to blend in with the frozen, snowy background.

HORNED LIZARD
The North American desert horned lizard shoots blood from its eyes to frighten away hungry predators.

BLACK BEAR
To hibernate for winter, the black bear's body fat increases for warmth. Its sleeping heart rate can slow from around fifty beats per minute to eight beats per minute.

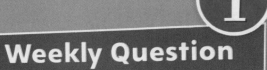

GILA WOODPECKERS

In the Sonoran Desert where trees are scarce, Gila woodpeckers make holes in the saguaro cactus, where they lay their eggs and raise their young. Other birds nest in abandoned holes.

Weekly Question

What different purposes do animal adaptations serve?

Quick Write Think of an animal you know of that has adapted to its environment. How has it adapted, and why? Illustrate the animal and freewrite your response.

I can learn more about informational text by analyzing the main idea and details.

Spotlight on Genre

Informational Text

Informational texts explain important ideas and tell facts about the world. Their characteristics include

- A **main idea** about a topic
- **Key details**, or factual information and evidence that support the main idea
- **Domain-specific vocabulary**, or words that are specific to the topic
- **Text and graphic features**, such as headings, maps, pictures, and diagrams, that help readers understand the text
- A clear **text structure**, or arrangement of information within a text

First, identify the topic of the text. Then, look for information about the topic.

TURN and TALK Describe to a partner an interesting fact or detail you learned from an informational text you have read. Take notes on your discussion.

My NOTES

Informational Text Anchor Chart

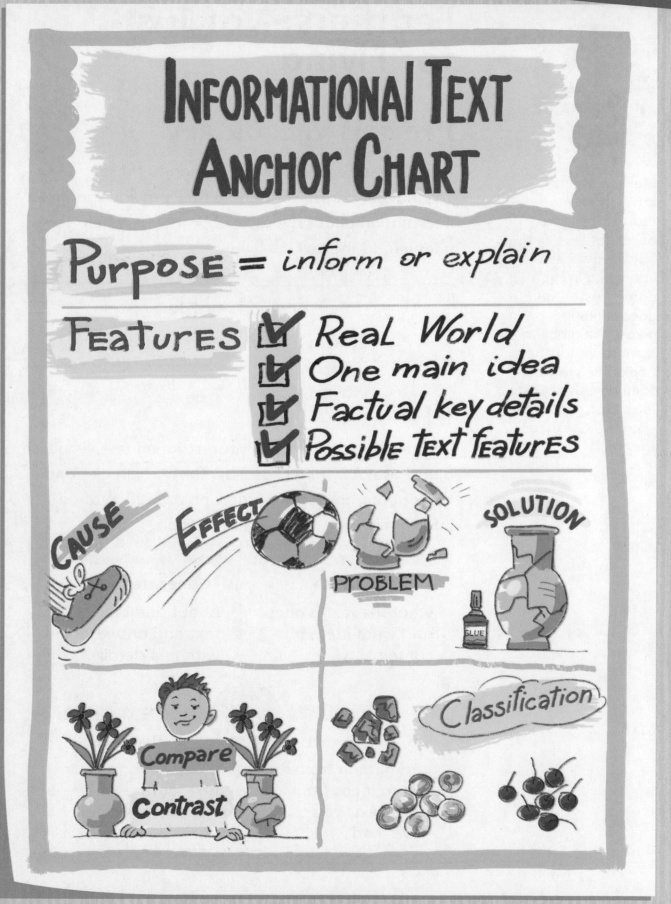

Purpose = inform or explain

Features
- ✓ Real World
- ✓ One main idea
- ✓ Factual key details
- ✓ Possible text features

CAUSE   EFFECT   PROBLEM   SOLUTION   GLUE

Compare   Contrast   Classification

Melissa Stewart has written more than 150 science books for kids. She has always been interested in the natural world and goes exploring across the globe to learn more for the books she writes. She has visited Costa Rica, East Africa, and even the Galápagos Islands!

Feathers: Not Just for Flying

Preview Vocabulary

As you read *Feathers*, pay attention to these vocabulary words. Notice how they provide specific information about the topic and how they help you understand the text.

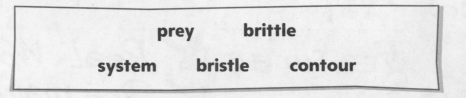

prey   brittle

system   bristle   contour

Read

Before you begin reading your assigned text, establish a purpose. As you read, follow these strategies and think about how each paragraph or section of an informational text relates to the topic.

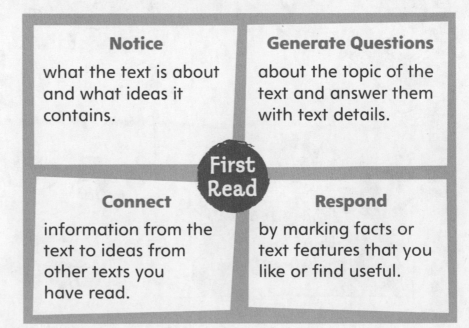

Notice what the text is about and what ideas it contains.

Generate Questions about the topic of the text and answer them with text details.

First Read

Connect information from the text to ideas from other texts you have read.

Respond by marking facts or text features that you like or find useful.

FEATHERS
Not Just for Flying

by Melissa Stewart

illustrated by Sarah S. Brannen

AUDIO

ANNOTATE

Analyze Main Idea and Details

Underline one word that tells the topic of the text. Then underline the main idea.

1   Birds and feathers go together, like trees and leaves, like stars and the sky. All birds have feathers, but no other animals do.

2   Most birds have thousands of feathers, but those feathers aren't all the same. That's because feathers have so many different jobs to do.

Feathers can warm like a blanket . . .

3   On cold, damp days a blue jay stays warm by fluffing up its feathers and trapping a layer of warm air next to its skin.

Blue jay, Bradbury Mountain, Maine

Wood duck, Lake Bemidji, Minnesota

or cushion like a pillow.

4   A female wood duck lines her nest with feathers she plucks from her own body. These feathers cushion the duck's eggs and keep them warm.

CLOSE READ

Analyze Main Idea and Details

Underline the details that tell more about the main idea.

Vocabulary in Context

Context clues are pieces of information around a term that can be used to determine or clarify the meanings of unfamiliar or multiple-meaning words. These clues can be in the text or in visuals.

Look for context clues in the illustration. Underline a word that refers to the blue, white, and rust appearance of the heron's feathers.

Feathers can shade out sun like an umbrella . . .

5   As a hungry tricolored heron wades through the water in search of food, it raises its wings high over its head. The feathers block out reflections from the sky and shade the water. This makes it easier to spot tasty fish and frogs.

Tricolored heron, Florida Everglades

Red-tailed hawk, Shiprock, New Mexico

or protect skin like sunscreen.

6   On sunny summer afternoons red-tailed hawks spend hours soaring through the sky in search of prey. Their thick feathers protect their delicate skin from the sun's harmful rays.

CLOSE READ

Monitor Comprehension

One way to clarify something, or make it clear, is by rereading a section and thinking about the details that support the main idea.

Highlight the reason a hawk's skin needs the protection of feathers.

prey an animal hunted by others for food

Analyze Main Idea and Details

Underline the details, or supporting evidence, that show why a male sandgrouse's feathers soak up water.

Feathers can soak up water like a sponge...

7   On sizzling summer days a male sandgrouse cools off by soaking his belly feathers in a watering hole. Then the proud papa flies to his nest. While dad guards his chicks, the little ones suck on his feathers to quench their thirst.

Pallas's sandgrouse, Gobi Desert, Mongolia

or clean up messes like a scrub brush.

8   An American bittern always cleans up after it eats. Its feathers have brittle tips that crumble into a dusty powder. The powder is perfect for scouring away the dirt and slimy fish oil that sticks to its feathers.

American bittern, Tualatin River, Oregon

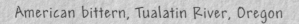

233

Analyze Main Idea and Details

Underline supporting evidence that explains why the dark-eyed junco has white tail feathers.

Feathers can distract attackers like a bullfighter's cape . . .

9   A dark-eyed junco distracts its enemies by flashing the bright white feathers on the outside of its tail. Then it quickly covers the feathers and darts off in the other direction.

Dark-eyed junco, Lincoln, Massachusetts

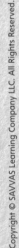

or hide a bird from predators like camouflage clothing.

10   A female cardinal's dull, grayish–tan body and feathers blend in with her forest home. They help her hide and protect her nest from enemies while she sits on her eggs.

Northern cardinal, Columbus, Ohio

CLOSE READ

Monitor Comprehension

One way to monitor your comprehension is to use background knowledge. Connect what you already know to details from the text.

Highlight a detail that relates to something you already know.

Analyze Main Idea and Details

Underline supporting evidence that explains why a manakin's feathers make sound.

Feathers can make high-pitched sounds like a whistle . . .

11   When a male club–winged manakin wants to get a female's attention, he leans forward, raises his wings over his back, and rapidly shakes them. As feathers with ridges rub against feathers with stiff, curved tips, a squeaky chirping sound trills through the air.

Club-winged manakin, Milpe Bird Sanctuary, Ecuador, South America

Peacock, Pusa Hill Forest, New Delhi, India

or attract attention like fancy jewelry.

12   A peacock's bright, beautiful tail feathers make him easy to spot. At mating time a female is attracted to the male with the biggest, most colorful fan of feathers.

CLOSE READ

Analyze Main Idea and Details

Underline evidence that tells why a male peacock's tail feathers attract a female.

Monitor Comprehension

Highlight a detail you do not understand. Then reread or read on for clues that help you understand.

Feathers can dig holes like a backhoe . . .

13   After bank swallows mate they make a home together. First the male uses his bill and the tough feathers on his lower legs to dig a two-foot-long tunnel in a stream bank. He pushes the dirt out with his wings. Then the female builds a nest of straw, grasses, and leaves at the end of the tunnel.

Bank swallow, Bear River, Utah

or carry building supplies like a forklift.

14   Most birds carry nesting materials in their beaks. But not the female rosy-faced lovebird. When she finds grass, leaves, or strips of bark, she tucks them under her rump feathers and flies back to her nest.

Rosy-faced Lovebird, Guab River, Namibia, Africa

CLOSE READ

Analyze Main Idea and Details

Underline phrases that Melissa Stewart uses to contrast the rosy-faced lovebird with other birds.

Analyze Main Idea and Details

Underline supporting evidence that explains how swans are able to float on the water's surface.

Feathers can help birds float like a life jacket . . .

15   Mute swans glide smoothly across the water's surface. Pockets of air trapped between their feathers help these graceful birds stay afloat.

Mute swan, Chesapeake Bay, Maryland

or plunge downward like a fishing sinker.

16   Most birds make a special oil to waterproof their feathers, but not the anhinga. The weight of its wet feathers helps the hungry hunter dive deep down in search of fish, crayfish, and shrimp.

Anhinga, Lake Martin, Louisiana

CLOSE READ

Analyze Main Idea and Details

Underline a phrase that shows how the anhinga's adaptation helps it survive.

Monitor Comprehension

Reread to clarify information. Highlight the detail that shows how emperor penguins are able to slide across ice and snow.

Feathers can glide like a sled . . .

17　Emperor penguins have tightly packed belly feathers that form firm, slick surfaces. The feathers make it easy for these birds to slide across ice and snow.

Emperor penguin, Adélie Land, Antarctica

or sprint across the snow like snowshoes.

18   Each autumn, willow ptarmigans grow a thick layer of feathers on top of their toes. Like snowshoes the feathers increase the size of the birds' feet, so they can shuffle across the snow instead of sinking in.

Willow ptarmigan, Denali National Park, Alaska

CLOSE READ

Analyze Main Idea and Details

<u>Underline</u> supporting evidence that explains why the willow ptarmigan's toe feathers are useful.

system set of connected things

bristle short and rough

But most of all, feathers can give birds the lift they need to race across the sky.

Kinds of Feathers

19 Many scientists study birds, and they are learning new information every day. Right now not all scientists agree about the best way to classify types of feathers. Here is one system that many scientists use:

20 Tiny filoplume feathers are attached to nerves. They help a bird sense its surroundings, and they let the bird know that its feathers are in place.

21 Stiff bristle feathers around a bird's eyes act like eyelashes. Some birds use bristle feathers around their mouths to locate food.

22 Soft, fluffy down feathers keep a bird warm by trapping body heat next to its skin.

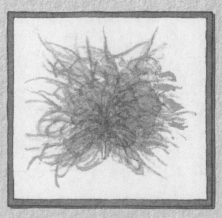

23   Semiplume feathers work with down feathers to keep birds warm and dry.

24   Contour feathers cover most of a bird's body. They give a bird its shape and colors.

25   The flight feathers on a bird's wings lift it up and move it forward. Flight feathers on the tail help a bird steer and keep its balance.

Analyze Main Idea and Details

Underline new purposes of feathers that Melissa Stewart introduces on this page.

contour related to the shape or outline of something

Develop Vocabulary

In informational text, authors use words that are specific to the topic. These words help the reader understand more about the topic.

My TURN Review the topic in the center circle. Then complete the graphic organizer by writing a word from the word bank in each circle and explaining how each word relates to the topic.

WORD BANK			
bristle	brittle	contour	system

This word relates to the topic because

This word relates to the topic because

Topic: feathers and how they are classified

brittle
This word relates to the topic because a brittle feather is a type of feather.

This word relates to the topic because

Check for Understanding

My TURN Look back at the text to answer the questions.

1. What clues tell you that *Feathers* is an informational text?

2. Identify the author's purpose in *Feathers*. How do the illustrations support this purpose?

3. Why does Melissa Stewart compare feathers to everyday objects? Cite text evidence to support an appropriate response.

4. What is the most surprising thing that feathers do? Write a brief argument to state and support your opinion.

Analyze Main Idea and Details

Authors include **details**, or facts and **supporting evidence**, to help develop the **main idea** in a text. You can analyze the evidence that Melissa Stewart includes to help you better understand the main idea.

1. **My TURN** Go to the Close Read notes in *Feathers*. Underline text that relates to the main idea and supporting evidence.

2. **Text Evidence** Use the parts you underlined to complete the chart.

Main Idea

Detail or Supporting Evidence	Detail or Supporting Evidence	Detail or Supporting Evidence

Monitor Comprehension

As you read, you **monitor comprehension,** or notice when you do not understand the text. Use strategies to increase your understanding. To reread, go back to the text and read a section again or a few times until you understand the ideas. To use background knowledge, connect the information from a text to information you learned before. To visualize, point out details in a text's images or illustrations, and use those details to understand information in the text.

1. **My TURN** Go back to the Close Read notes and highlight details you did not understand.

2. **Text Evidence** Use your highlighted evidence to complete the chart.

What I did not understand	The comprehension strategy I used	What I understand now
"Feathers can dig holes like a backhoe"	I used the reread strategy. I read the section again to understand the ideas.	Bank swallows use their feathers like construction tools to dig holes.

How did comprehension strategies help you understand the main idea?

_____

_____

Reflect and Share

Talk About It In *Feathers*, Melissa Stewart describes the many ways birds use their feathers. Think about all the texts you have read this week. What other living things have you read about? What characteristics help them survive? Use these questions to help you express an opinion about why animals must adapt.

Express an Opinion When giving your opinion, express your ideas clearly so that others can understand.

- ◎ Make eye contact with other people in your group.
- ◎ Speak at a natural rate and volume.
- ◎ Use details from the text to clarify your points and respond to questions your partners ask.

Use these sentence starters to guide your responses:

I think it is important for animals to adapt because . . .

The part in *Feathers* that best supports my opinion is . . .

Based on information in _____ , I think . . .

Weekly Question

What different purposes do animal adaptations serve?

Academic Vocabulary

Related words are words that are connected. Related words can have similar word parts such as *auto* in *automatic* and *automotive*. Related words can also have connected meanings such as the words *barrier* and *obstacle*. Both can be used to describe something that prevents movement or progress.

Learning Goal

I can develop knowledge about language to make connections between reading and writing.

My TURN To complete the web,

1. **Read** the academic vocabulary words related to the topic.

2. **Write** a reason the word is connected to the topic.

3. **Add** other words that are connected to the topic. Write a reason they are connected to the topic.

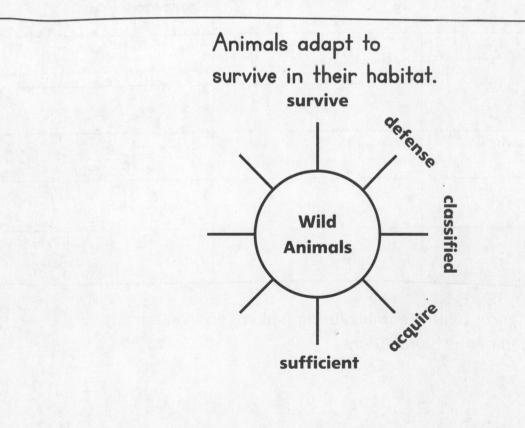

Animals adapt to
survive in their habitat.

survive

defense

classified

acquire

sufficient

Wild Animals

Plurals

A **plural** noun refers to two or more people, places, or things. Usually, a noun can be changed from singular to plural by adding -s. In plural nouns, the letter s usually spells the sound z, as in the word *homes*. Singular nouns that end in *ch*, *sh*, *s*, *ss*, or *x* can be made plural by adding -es to the end. Adding -es to a noun adds a syllable to the base word, as in the word *dishes*. Plural nouns formed by adding -s or -es are called regular plurals.

My TURN Read each regular plural noun. Then complete the chart.

Plural Noun	Add Ending -s or -es?	Singular Noun
systems	–s	system
brushes		
eyelashes		
herons		
foxes		
feathers		

Write two sentences about *Feathers*, using a plural noun in each sentence. Underline the plural nouns.

_____

_____

Read Like a Writer

Authors use graphic features, such as illustrations and diagrams, to achieve specific purposes. Graphic features support the main idea and help readers understand complex information.

Model ! Read this text from *Feathers*, and look at the illustration that goes with paragraph 3.

> On cold, damp days a blue jay stays warm by fluffing up its feathers and trapping a layer of warm air next to its skin.

1. **Identify** The main idea of the paragraph is that a blue jay uses its feathers to stay warm.

2. **Question** How does the illustration with paragraph 3 help me understand the main idea?

3. **Conclude** The illustration shows strands of yarn woven into a piece of fabric. This helps me understand that a jay's feathers act like a blanket to keep it warm in the cold.

Reread paragraph 5, and look at the illustration that goes with it.

My TURN Follow the steps to analyze how the illustration connects with the author's purpose.

1. **Identify** The main idea of the paragraph is _____

2. **Question** How does the illustration achieve the author's purpose?

3. **Conclude** The illustration _____

Write for a Reader

Illustrations help an author show key aspects of a main idea.

Authors use graphic features to help readers understand ideas in a text. Illustrations, in particular, can show readers exactly what the author describes in other parts of a text.

My TURN Think about how the illustrations Melissa Stewart included in *Feathers* helped you understand the main idea. Now, consider how you can use a graphic feature to support a main idea of your own.

1. If you were writing about an animal with a unique adaptation, what graphic feature would you include to help readers understand that adaptation?

_____

_____

_____

2. Write your main idea about the animal adaptation. Tell what graphic feature you would include, and explain how it supports your main idea.

Main idea:

_____

_____

Graphic feature:

_____

_____

_____

_____

_____

Spell Plurals

Plural nouns can be spelled by adding -s to a singular noun. Singular nouns that end in *ch*, *sh*, *s*, *ss*, or *x* can be made plural by adding -es to the end. Singular nouns ending in *y* that comes after a consonant become plural by changing the *y* to an *i* and adding -es. For singular nouns ending in a *y* that comes after a vowel, add *s* to make the noun plural.

My TURN Read the words. Sort and spell them by the spelling rules they follow.

SPELLING WORDS			
services	primaries	consumers	holidays
lenses	sandwiches	monkeys	berries
counties	taxes	hoaxes	classes
gases	viruses	speeches	skies
activities	colonies	galaxies	victories

Added -s

_____

_____

_____

_____

_____

_____

Added -es

_____

_____

_____

_____

_____

_____

Changed y to i and added -es

_____

_____

_____

_____

_____

_____

Compound Sentences

A **compound sentence** is a sentence that contains two simple sentences joined by a comma and a coordinating conjunction, or joining word, such as *and*, *but*, and *or*. Writers use compound sentences to add sentence variety to their writing and make the writing flow smoothly.

- *And* combines related ideas.
- *But* combines contrasting ideas.
- *Or* combines related but alternative ideas.

Simple Sentences	Joining Word	Compound Sentence
Most birds have thousands of feathers. Those feathers are not all the same.	*but*	Most birds have thousands of feathers, **but** those feathers are not all the same.
A female cardinal has dull feathers. A male cardinal has bright ones.	*and*	A female cardinal has dull feathers, **and** a male cardinal has bright ones.
Feathers can warm like a blanket. Feathers can cushion like a pillow.	*or*	Feathers can warm like a blanket, **or** they can cushion like a pillow.

My TURN Edit this draft by combining sentences using coordinating conjunctions.

Some birds' feathers keep them warm. Other birds' feathers protect their skin like sunscreen. For example, the blue jay uses fluffed-up feathers to stay warm. The red-tailed hawk uses its feathers to protect its skin from the sun's rays.

Analyze a Travel Article

A travel article is an informational text about a place readers might want to visit. To convey an idea about a place, the writer chooses details and organizes the article to appeal to an audience.

Like all articles, a travel article has a **headline**, or a catchy title that draws readers in. The first paragraph, or **lead,** includes the main idea and the most important information. The body of the article includes details readers should know. At the end of the article, the writer provides information that is interesting but not essential for people who want to visit the place.

My TURN Study a travel article from your classroom library. In your writing notebook, use the diagram to copy the headline and briefly summarize the content of each section.

Headline _____

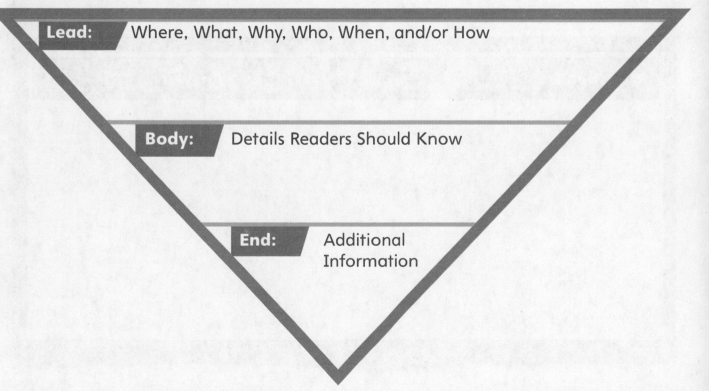

Lead: Where, What, Why, Who, When, and/or How

Body: Details Readers Should Know

End: Additional Information

257

Analyze a Lead Paragraph

The **lead** in a travel article quickly tells a main idea about a place. It answers the questions *Who, What, Where, When, Why,* and *How.* A successful lead paragraph makes readers want to keep reading.

My TURN Examine the first paragraph of a travel article you have read. Identify two of the questions that it answers. Write the questions on the left. On the right, summarize how the lead paragraph answers each question.

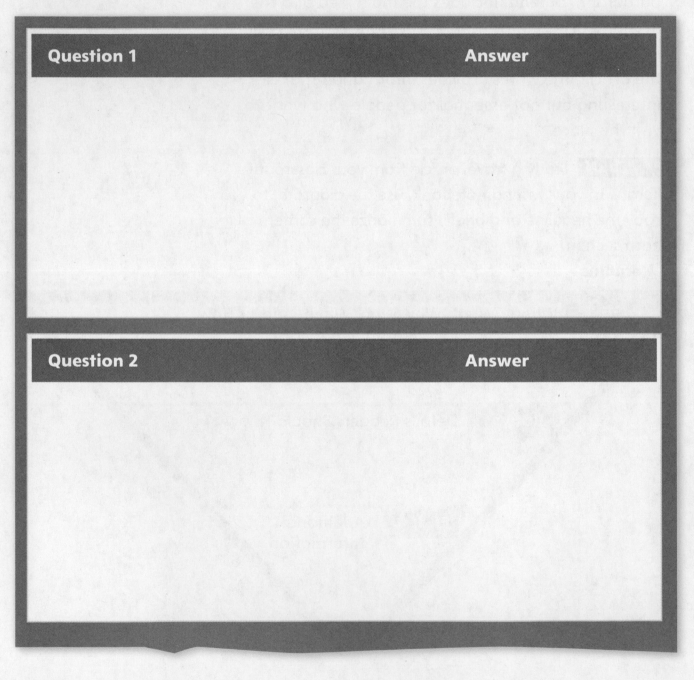

Question 1	Answer

Question 2	Answer

Analyze Photographs

A place to visit is called a **destination**. A travel article includes many details about a destination. The article usually includes attractive photographs of the destination too. These photographs entice readers by showing what the place looks like and focusing on the visual beauty or interest of a place. Travel writers use photographs to further encourage their readers to visit the destination.

My TURN Work with a partner. From your classroom library, choose two travel articles that contain photographs. Describe the pictures in the boxes below. Then answer the questions.

Photographs in Article 1	Photographs in Article 2

1. Which article appeals to you more, Article 1 or Article 2?

_____

2. How do the photographs add detail to the article? Explain how that detail influences your preference.

_____

_____

_____

Brainstorm and Set a Purpose

The process of gathering ideas is called **brainstorming.** During brainstorming, writers record everything that comes to mind without filtering or judging. To brainstorm, ask: What topics interest me? What do I already know about those topics? What is my purpose for writing? What audience might read my writing? What might they already know about the topic?

My TURN In your writing notebook, brainstorm about three destinations. Write down the first thoughts you have about each one. Then highlight your favorite one to identify the topic you choose for your travel article.

- Determine your **purpose** for writing. Are you writing to inform, to persuade, or to entertain?
- Analyze your **audience.** Think about who will read your writing and why.

My TURN Next, identify a purpose and audience for your travel article.

My **purpose** is _____.

My **audience** is _____.

Your enthusiasm will help your readers get excited about the topic, too!

Plan Your Travel Article

An article includes a clear main idea and facts the writer has chosen depending on the purpose and audience. The writer may choose to exclude, or leave out, some facts. To write a well-organized article, the writer must carefully select details to include.

My TURN Identify a main idea for your travel article. In the left column, highlight two facts related to your main idea that you will emphasize in the lead. In the right column, list the main information your audience needs to learn about your destination from the body of the article. Discuss your plan with your Writing Club.

Lead	Body Information
Where the place is	1.
What is special there	
	2.
Who should visit	
When people should visit	3.
Why people should visit	
	4.
How people can get there	

SURVIVAL
Adaptations

Camouflage is an adaptation that allows animals to blend into their environment. This adaptation can increase an animal's chances for survival. Many species have developed different ways to camouflage themselves.

For example, the pygmy seahorse has the same coloring and markings as the coral that lives in the western Pacific Ocean. The pygmy seahorse uses its appearance to hide in the coral and away from its predators.

Watch the video to find the hidden animal. Notice how the movement, sound, and visuals in the video help you understand how animals use camouflage. Then look at the images and read the captions.

 Watch

A flounder's flat body disappears into the seafloor. Its adaptation allows it to hunt for food as well as hide from predators.

Weekly Question

How do adaptations help animals survive?

TURN and TALK How are the text and media related? Recognize characteristics of this text that help you understand how animals use camouflage.

Then use details from the text to explain how camouflage helps animals survive.

The natterjack toad uses its coloring to blend into the environment.

Look closely. Do you see the leopard hiding? Animals that have spots or stripes use their patterns to blend into the background.

Learning Goal

I can learn more about informational text by analyzing cause-and-effect text structure.

Spotlight on Genre

Informational Text

Authors organize **informational texts** to demonstrate the relationships between ideas and details. Some common text structures, or organizational patterns, are

- **Cause and Effect:** effects and possible causes for each effect
- **Chronological Order:** events in the order they happened
- **Problem and Solution:** a problem and one or more solutions
- **Compare and Contrast:** similarities and differences between two or more events, people, or ideas
- **Description** or **Classification:** describes or explains different aspects of a topic

Establish Purpose One purpose for reading informational text is to learn more about a topic. Setting a purpose for reading can help you focus and monitor your comprehension as you read.

How does a text show relationships? Answering this will help you determine the text structure.

My PURPOSE

_____

_____

_____

TURN and TALK Share your purpose for reading *Animal Mimics* with a partner. Explain why you chose your purpose, supporting your ideas with examples and details. Then listen actively and make thoughtful comments when your partner shares.

✻ INFORMATIONAL TEXT: TEXT STRUCTURE ANCHOR CHART ✻

TEXT STRUCTURE	SIGNAL WORDS	GRAPHIC ORGANIZER
Cause and Effect 👉	Because Since Therefore If...then As a result	Causes — Effects Why did it happen? → What happened?
Chronological Order 👉	First Next Finally Then	event 1 event 2 event 3
Problem and Solution 👉	Solve In order to So that Since Therefore	
Compare and Contrast 👉	Also But However Both Yet	
Description or Classification 👉	For example For instance Such as	

Meet the Author

Marie Racanelli is the author of several other books about animals, including *Underground Animals* and *Camouflaged Creatures*.

Animal Mimics

Preview Vocabulary

As you read *Animal Mimics*, pay attention to these vocabulary words. Notice how they help you understand the text.

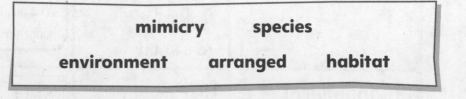

> mimicry   species
>
> environment   arranged   habitat

Read

Before you read *Animal Mimics*, scan the text to look at its structure, or how it is organized. Based on what you notice, make a prediction about what the text will be about. Record your prediction and keep it in mind as you read.

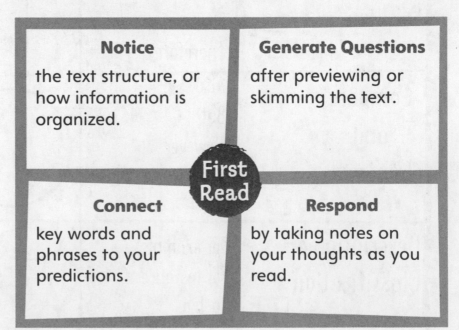

Notice the text structure, or how information is organized.

Generate Questions after previewing or skimming the text.

First Read

Connect key words and phrases to your predictions.

Respond by taking notes on your thoughts as you read.

Animal Mimics

by Marie Racanelli

AUDIO

ANNOTATE

Analyze Text Structure

Underline two sentences that describe causes. Then underline a sentence that describes the effect.

mimicry the ability to look or act like something else

species categories of living things

Confirm or Correct Predictions

Based on the visuals and the heading, what do you predict this section will be about? Highlight text evidence that helps you confirm or correct a prediction about the main idea in the section "What Is Mimicry?"

What Is Mimicry?

1   There are thousands of animals in our world. Some of these animals are predators, and some of them will end up as prey. They all need to eat. They all need to keep themselves safe. Some animals, over time, have adapted certain features that match those of other species. These features fool their predators and help the animals live longer. These animals are called mimics.

2   Mimics copy the appearance, action, or sound of another animal that predators fear or do not like to eat. The animals they copy are called models. Let's learn more about these copycats in nature.

The caterpillar of the spicebush swallowtail butterfly looks like a snake or lizard because of the shape of its back and the eyespots.

Analyze Text Structure

Some animals look like other animals. <u>Underline</u> one effect of their appearance.

environment all the living things and conditions of a place

Confirm or Correct Predictions

Highlight text evidence that helps you confirm or correct a prediction about the hoverfly's appearance.

Copycat!

3   There are different kinds of mimicry. One kind is called Batesian mimicry. It is named after Henry Walter Bates, a naturalist. He discovered that some weaker animals adapted to their environment by copying or looking like dangerous animals. These weaker animals often have no defenses, such as stingers or poisons. Instead, they look very much like other animals that do, and so their enemies leave them alone.

4   One example of Batesian mimicry is the hoverfly. Over time this fly has adapted to have yellow and black stripes like a bee. Animals know that a bee will sting them, so they leave this kind of fly alone.

The hoverfly, or flower fly, not only looks like a bee or wasp, but it also drinks nectar, as bees do. These flies cannot sting, as bees do, though.

Analyze Text Structure

<u>Underline</u> a reason why predators rarely attack king and milk snakes.

arranged organized or designed

Confirm or Correct Predictions

Highlight text evidence that helps you confirm or correct a prediction about how mimicry helps king and milk snakes.

A Closer Look at Batesian Mimicry

5   Coral, king, and milk snakes are excellent examples of Batesian mimicry. Coral snakes are poisonous. King and milk snakes are not. Coral snakes have colorful scales in bands of black, red, and yellow. The yellow bands always touch the red ones. These colors announce the snakes' deadly poison. Some king and milk snakes also have bands of red, black, and yellow, but they are arranged in a different order.

6   It is not always easy to tell these snakes apart. A predator will often leave king or milk snakes alone because it sees their colors and believes that they are poisonous, too.

This king snake (above) has adapted its coloring as a defense. Predators see bands like those of the coral snake (below) and leave the snake alone.

Copyright © SAVVAS Learning Company LLC. All Rights Reserved.

Analyze Text Structure

<u>Underline</u> details about what causes birds to stay away from both monarch and viceroy butterflies.

Confirm or Correct Predictions

Highlight text evidence that helps you confirm or correct a prediction about mimicry.

Eat at Your Own Risk!

7   Another type of mimicry is called Müllerian mimicry. It is named after Fritz Müller, a German zoologist. Müllerian mimicry occurs when animals from different species look alike and are either poisonous or bad tasting. Generally these animals are brightly colored. The colors are a warning sign to predators that the animals should be left alone.

8   Monarch and viceroy butterflies are good examples of Müllerian mimicry. Their colors and the markings on their wings look alike. The monarch is poisonous and the viceroy tastes very bad. A bird that has tried either one will likely stay away from both.

The bad-tasting viceroy, shown here, mimics the poisonous monarch. Birds that have tasted one butterfly with this coloring are unlikely to try another one.

Analyze Text Structure

Underline a signal word or phrase that helps you find important information about Müllerian mimicry.

Confirm or Correct Predictions

Highlight text evidence that helps you confirm or correct a prediction about Müllerian mimicry.

A Closer Look at Müllerian Mimicry

9   Another good example of Müllerian mimicry is the poison dart frog, in South America and Central America, and the Mantella frog, from Madagascar. The bright colors of both species warn predators of their toxic, or poisonous, skin. The frogs are small but highly poisonous. Their enemies generally stay far away from them and any other frogs with bright colors.

10   The indigenous people who live in the rain forest sometimes use the frog's toxin when they go hunting. They rub the tips of their arrows or darts on the skin of one or two frogs. This is why the frogs are known as poison dart or poison arrow frogs.

Though not all poison dart frogs look alike, they all have brightly colored skin. These bright colors let predators know the animal is poisonous.

Crazy Copycat Facts!

1. Mimicry happens in both plants and animals.

2. Certain ant-eating spiders mimic ants and this makes it easier for them to enter an ant colony.

3. Some birds, such as parrots and mockingbirds, mimic other birds' songs and sometimes other sounds, such as car alarms or voices.

4. Most mimics are insects, such as butterflies and moths, but mimicry also appears in spiders, snakes, frogs, fish, and other animals.

5. Chances of staying safe from predators increase when there are more models than mimics in a group.

6. Hoverflies, which look like honeybees, even make a sound like a bee makes when predators are near.

7. A few rhymes have been made up to help people tell the difference between coral snakes and their mimics. One example is, "If red touches yellow, avoid this fellow."

8. Hawk-moth caterpillars tuck in their heads, bend their bodies, show off their eyespots, and mimic snakes. They even wiggle from side to side to look more like a snake!

Analyze Text Structure

Underline information that tells you something new about mimicry.

CLOSE READ

Analyze Text Structure

Underline information that supports the author's purpose.

Confirm or Correct Predictions

Highlight text evidence that helps you confirm or correct a prediction about the way animals use mimicry.

What Is Self-Mimicry?

11   Have you ever looked at a caterpillar and wondered which end was its head? Some animals have a type of defense called self-mimicry. These creatures often have body parts that mimic other parts of their own bodies. Some of these animals have markings called eyespots.

12   Self-mimicry is not used only by prey. Sometimes predators, such as frogmouth catfish, use self-mimicry, too. A frogmouth catfish has something on its tongue that looks like food other fish like to eat. The catfish lies very still, sticking out its long tongue. When a small fish approaches the "food," the catfish quickly eats the fish!

The longlure frogfish hides itself among sponges and moves a body part that looks like food. When a fish swims over for lunch, it gets eaten instead!

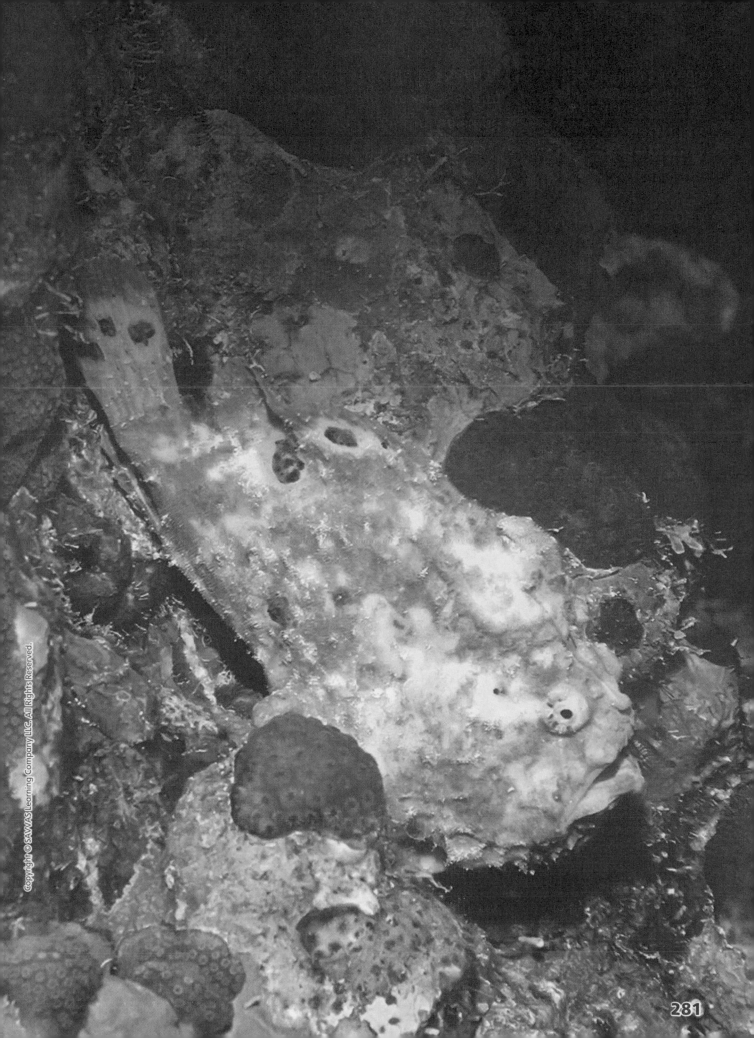

Analyze Text Structure

Underline the most important details about eyespots.

Confirm or Correct Predictions

Highlight text evidence that helps you confirm or correct a prediction about how animals use eyespots.

More About Eyespots

13 Some species of butterflies, moths, fish, frogs, and caterpillars have large circles on their bodies. These circles are called eyespots because they look like eyes.

14 Predators generally like to approach their prey without being seen. Eyespots confuse predators and they come toward their prey from the wrong side. The prey sees them coming and has time to escape.

15 Eyespots can keep animals safe in another way, too. Some animals, such as lo moths, hawk-moth caterpillars, and false-eyed frogs, have markings that look like the eyes of a big animal. These "eyes" scare away predators.

The owl butterfly gets its name from the large eyespots on its wings, which look like the eyes of an owl.

Analyze Text Structure

<u>Underline</u> the most important details about body-part mimics.

Confirm or Correct Predictions

Highlight text evidence that helps you confirm or correct a prediction about how animals use body-part mimicry.

More About Body-Part Mimics

16   Let's take a closer look at the animals that mimic another body part. This form of mimicry helps animals draw attention away from important body parts, such as the head. Predators will likely bite a part of the body that will not hurt the prey as much.

17   There are some snakes that have tails that look like their heads or heads that look like their tails. This mimicry saves the snake because a bird trying to eat the snake might not bite the head. The bird could also miss catching the snake if it starts moving in the opposite direction from what the bird expected.

Can you tell which end is the head on this caterpillar? With luck, a bird will not be able to spot the head easily either!

Why Is Mimicry Important?

18 Mimicry helps an animal live longer in its habitat, which is the goal of most animals. Over time, animals that looked like something that scared off or confused predators lived. The animals that did not have these special colors or markings did not.

19 At the same time, the predators have adapted, too. They have learned which animals might hurt them and they stay away from those animals. Changing when the environment changes is key to a species' survival over time. Mimicry is just one of the many tools animals have adapted to live in our ever-changing natural world!

Glossary

adapted (uh-DAPT-ed) Changed to fit requirements.

dangerous (DAYN-jeh-rus) Might cause hurt.

defenses (dih-FENS-uhz) Things a living thing has or does that help keep it safe.

environment (en-VY-ern-ment) All the living things and conditions of a place.

indigenous (in-DIH-jeh-nus) Having started in and coming naturally from a certain place.

mimics (MIH-miks) Things that copy something else closely.

poisons (POY-zunz) Things that cause pain or death.

predators (PREH-duh-terz) Animals that kill other animals for food.

prey (PRAY) An animal that is hunted by another animal for food.

scales (SKAYLZ) The thin, dry pieces of skin that form the outer covering of snakes, lizards, and other reptiles.

species (SPEE-sheez) One kind of living thing. All people are one species.

toxin (TOK-sun) A type of poison.

Develop Vocabulary

In informational texts, authors use specific words that are related to the topic they are writing about. They use these words to explain ideas and clarify relationships between ideas.

My TURN Make connections between the pairs of vocabulary words by answering the questions.

environment and habitat

1. Why can there be more than one **habitat** in a single **environment?**

_____

_____

_____

mimicry and species

2. In what way can **mimicry** be good for a **species?**

_____

_____

_____

species and arranged

3. How does the way their scale colors are **arranged** help king and milk snake **species?**

_____

_____

_____

Check for Understanding

My TURN Look back at the text to answer the questions.

1. What examples from *Animal Mimics* tell you that it is an informational text?

2. Why does Marie Racanelli choose to explain mimicry and self-mimicry in the same text? What is similar about the two topics? Cite text evidence.

3. What do all the ideas about mimicry in Marie Racanelli's text have in common?

4. Which animal's mimicry do you think is the most effective? Choose one animal and write a brief argument explaining your opinion.

Analyze Text Structure

Text structure is the organizational pattern an author uses to arrange information in a text. Recognizing a text's structure can help you find the main idea. An author uses **cause-and-effect** text structure to explain reasons why something happens (the cause) and what happens as a result (the effect).

1. **My TURN** Go to the Close Read notes in *Animal Mimics*. Underline parts that help you understand how Marie Racanelli uses a cause-and-effect text structure to achieve her purpose.

2. **Text Evidence** Use the parts you underlined to complete the graphic organizer.

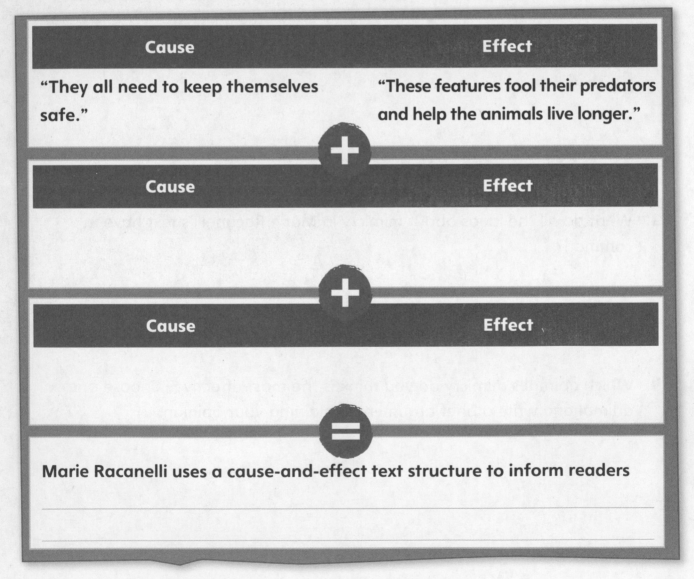

Cause	Effect
"They all need to keep themselves safe."	"These features fool their predators and help the animals live longer."

+

Cause	Effect

+

Cause	Effect

=

Marie Racanelli uses a cause-and-effect text structure to inform readers

Confirm or Correct Predictions

To make predictions about a text use what you know about the genre and its structure and features. In nonfiction, genre features like headings and visuals can help you make and confirm or correct predictions. As you read, confirm or correct your predictions by using the structure and features of the text. Find facts and details that help you correct or confirm your predictions.

1. **My TURN** Think about the predictions you made before reading *Animal Mimics*. Then go back to the Close Read notes and highlight details that helped you confirm or correct your predictions.

2. **Text Evidence** Write your predictions and details in the chart.

Prediction

Confirmed or Corrected?

Prediction

Confirmed or Corrected?

Reflect and Share

Write to Sources Animals use adaptations such as mimicry to stay safe from predators. How has learning about animal survival helped you understand how wild animals behave? Use examples from the texts you read this week to write and support a response. Use the following writing process to compare and contrast information.

Compare and Contrast Ideas Comparing and contrasting ideas from different sources allows writers to evaluate ideas from various texts and draw their own conclusions.

Before you write your response, take notes about texts you have read. For each text, answer the following questions in your notes.

- ◐ What animals have I learned about?
- ◐ How do these animals avoid predators?
- ◐ How are these survival strategies similar to or different from those used by other animals I have read about?

Now use the information to write a response. Remember to cite evidence from the different sources by using direct quotations or paraphrasing information.

> ## Weekly Question

How do adaptations help animals survive?

Academic Vocabulary

Synonyms and antonyms have meanings that are related. Synonyms are words that have similar meanings. Antonyms are words with opposite meanings. Thinking about the relationships between words can help readers better understand their specific meanings.

My TURN For each word in the center column,

1. **Write** a short definition, using a glossary or dictionary if needed.

2. **Write** two synonyms. Write one antonym.

3. **Confirm** your responses using a thesaurus.

Synonyms	Words	Antonyms
develop earn	acquire to gain over time	lose
	classified	
	defense	
	sufficient	
	survive	

Vowel Diphthongs

Diphthongs are vowel teams that work together to spell a different sound. The vowel teams *ou, ow, oi, oy* are diphthongs.

The vowel sound you hear in the word *out* can be spelled *ou* or *ow*. The vowel sound you hear in the word *joy* can be spelled *oi* or *oy*. Learning these sound-spelling patterns can help you read words with diphthongs.

My TURN Use these activities to apply your knowledge of vowel diphthongs.

1. Read these words with diphthongs: *account, choicest, boyhood, browser, outline, coward, decoy, poison.*

2. Write 3 sentences that include at least one word with a vowel diphthong.

_____

_____

_____

High-Frequency Words

High-frequency words are words that you will see in texts over and over again. They often do not follow regular word study patterns. Read these high-frequency words: *metal, instruments, paragraphs, clothes, design, appear.* Try to identify them in your independent reading.

Read Like a Writer

Text features, such as headings and captions, organize ideas and help readers locate information. Headings locate and identify important ideas. Captions often add interesting and important information about an image in a text.

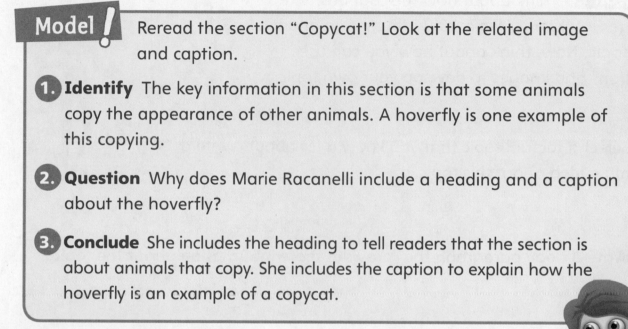

Model ! Reread the section "Copycat!" Look at the related image and caption.

1. **Identify** The key information in this section is that some animals copy the appearance of other animals. A hoverfly is one example of this copying.

2. **Question** Why does Marie Racanelli include a heading and a caption about the hoverfly?

3. **Conclude** She includes the heading to tell readers that the section is about animals that copy. She includes the caption to explain how the hoverfly is an example of a copycat.

Reread the section "Eat at Your Own Risk!" Look at the related image and caption.

My TURN Follow the steps to connect the heading and caption with the passage.

1. **Identify** The key information is that _____

_____

2. **Question** Why does Marie Racanelli include a heading and a caption about the viceroy?

3. **Conclude** She includes the heading to tell readers _____

_____

She includes the caption to explain _____

_____

Write for a Reader

Authors use text features, such as headings and captions, to add extra information related to the topic.

Captions and images help an author add interesting information about a topic.

My TURN Think about how the captions and images in *Animal Mimics* add information about the topic. Now, think about how you can use captions and images to develop your own topic.

1. Select a factual topic that you know a lot about. Write a main idea about this topic.

_____

2. Write a body paragraph that provides more information about the topic.

_____

_____

_____

_____

3. How could you use text features to organize and add to your topic? Write a few caption and image ideas that could help develop your topic.

Caption Ideas	Image Ideas

Spell Vowel Diphthongs

Vowel diphthongs are two letters that spell one, different sound. The letters *ou, ow* can spell the vowel sound you hear in the word *cow*. The letters *oi, oy* spell the vowel sound you hear in the word *boy*. Remember these spelling patterns as you edit the spelling in your own writing.

My TURN Read the words. Then spell and alphabetize them. Make sure to spell each vowel diphthong, or vowel team, correctly.

SPELLING WORDS			
coward	boundary	foundation	announce
boycott	voyage	exploit	poison
toil	decoy	scrounge	moist
choice	boil	ouch	scout
allow	sour	browser	outline

_____   _____

_____   _____

_____   _____

_____   _____

_____   _____

_____   _____

_____   _____

_____   _____

My TURN When you edit drafts of your writing, check to make sure that you used the patterns for vowel diphthongs to correctly spell words.

Complex Sentences

A group of words with a subject and a verb is called a clause. An **independent clause** can stand alone as a sentence. A **dependent clause** begins with a word such as *because*, *if*, or *when*. It cannot stand alone as a sentence.

A **complex sentence** has a dependent clause and an independent clause. When the dependent clause comes first, the clause is followed by a comma.

Independent Clause	Dependent Clause	Complex Sentence
the flatfish buries parts of its body in the sand and mud	when it hunts for prey	The flatfish buries parts of its body in the sand and mud when it hunts for prey.
it is fooled by the fish's false eyes	if a predator tries to sneak up on a four-eye butterfly fish	If a predator tries to sneak up on a four-eye butterfly fish, it is fooled by the fish's false eyes.

My TURN Edit this draft by combining independent and dependent clauses to create complex sentences.

Some animals use other animals to protect themselves. If young fish need a place to hide. They use jellyfish to their advantage. Jellyfish have stinging tentacles. Young fish hide in these tentacles. Because predators are too scared to come near them. When the young fish get bigger. It leave the jellyfish.

Develop an Introduction

Learning Goal

I can use elements of informational text to write an article.

The introduction of a travel article is called the **lead.** The lead grabs readers' interest with basic facts about the **destination**, or the place the article describes. A successful lead includes a clear main idea and is just one or two short paragraphs. It makes readers want to keep reading.

My TURN Use the chart to develop ideas for an introduction, or lead paragraph, of a travel article.

Questions Answered in a Lead	Answers About My Destination
Who should visit? When should they visit?	
What is special here?	
Where is the place? How can people get here?	
Why should people visit?	

My TURN Use the completed chart to develop and compose a travel article in your writing notebook. Be sure to include a clear main idea about your destination.

The lead of a travel article should attract readers.

Develop Relevant Details

The **main topic** of a travel article is a specific place called the destination. The **focus** of a travel article is what makes the destination a good place to visit. **Relevant details** are directly related to the main topic and focus of the article. Irrelevant details are about another topic or distract readers from the focus of the article.

My TURN Read the headline and article. Cross out irrelevant details to create more focused paragraphs.

Visit New Orleans to Run with the Bulls!

You may think a trip to Spain is the only way to see the Running of the Bulls, but an opportunity to see it may be closer than you think. Every July, New Orleans hosts its own Running of the Bulls. Of course, it is hot in a lot of places in July. If you can go to a swimming pool, you are lucky!

As they are year-round, New Orleans music and food are great. The annual Running of the Bulls festival is named for the one in Spain, where bulls run through the streets. In New Orleans, the runners are people from roller derby teams! I really like roller derbies. The roller-skating "bulls" in New Orleans sign up for the festival and chase one another in large groups.

My TURN Develop relevant details for your travel article in your writing notebook.

Develop Different Types of Details

Authors use a variety of relevant details to write an engaging article.

- **facts:** information proven as true
- **definitions:** meanings of words
- **concrete details:** precise names and descriptions
- **quotations:** comments or questions people make
- **examples:** specific people, places, or things that support a fact or claim

My TURN Compose a paragraph for a travel article using the details below. On the lines, number each detail to show the order in which you would like each detail to appear.

_____ Fresh fruit in the market includes avocados, bananas, lychees, mangoes, and papayas. (examples of fresh fruit)

_____ A lychee is a small fruit with a thin shell and one large seed. (definition)

_____ To eat a lychee, peel away the bumpy red skin to reveal the cool, white fruit, but do not eat the large brown seed inside. (concrete detail)

_____ Lychees grow on lychee trees, which scientists classify in the same group as maple and horse chestnut trees. (fact)

_____ "Nothing tastes like lychee straight from the tree!" my aunt exclaimed. (quotation)

My TURN Develop different types of details to use in your travel article in your writing notebook.

Compose Captions for Visuals

Travel articles often include maps and photographs. A map will have a title and labels that name what the map shows. A **caption** is a sentence or two that tells what a photograph shows. In a travel article, the captions usually describe features that will attract visitors.

My TURN Write captions for the photographs.

Clear skies and blue water guarantee a relaxing visit.

My TURN Compose captions for the visuals you use in your travel article.

An interesting travel photo makes people want to read the caption, and an interesting caption makes people want to read the article.

Develop a Conclusion

A travel article is organized like an upside-down pyramid. The first paragraph includes information readers need the most. The last paragraph focuses on information readers might find interesting but unnecessary to understand the article.

To conclude a travel article, the writer may

- give an opinion about visiting the destination.
- refer readers to other sources of information.
- remind readers of the top reason for visiting the destination.

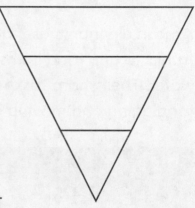

My TURN Use this list to select relevant details you would include in the conclusion of a travel article about the nation's capital, Washington, D.C.

Yes	No	Include in the Concluding Paragraph
		The average July temperature is 87°F.
		To see government at work, visit any state capitol building.
		Get a free official visitors guide through the Destination DC Web site.
		In my opinion, a walk through the National Mall is a lesson in U.S. history.
		You can spend several days visiting monuments, memorials, and museums.

My TURN In your writing notebook, develop a conclusion for your travel article that follows this structure and focuses on relevant details.

WEEKLY LAUNCH: PRIMARY SOURCE

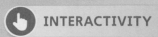 INTERACTIVITY

SAVING
Elephants

African elephants use their long trunks to grip food items and suck up water. Their sharp tusks are useful for digging and moving objects.

Elephant tusks are made of ivory, which is considered very valuable. Ivory has been carved into artwork and traded like money. Because of ivory's value, elephants are illegally hunted for their tusks.

Conservation organizations work with governments to pass laws that help protect elephants. Although elephants are still endangered, people are working hard to save them.

from **African Elephant Conservation Act of 1989**

4201. *Statement of purpose* The purpose of this title is to perpetuate healthy populations of African elephants.

4202. *Congressional* The Congress finds the following:

1. Elephant populations in Africa have declined at an alarming rate since the mid-1970's.

2. The large illegal trade in African elephant ivory is the major cause of this decline and threatens the continued existence of the African elephant.

3. The African elephant is listed as threatened under the Endangered Species Act of 1973 . . . and its continued existence will be further jeopardized if this decline is not reversed.

Weekly Question

What challenges do animals face in their environments?

TURN and TALK What animals, besides elephants, are in danger or threatened in their environments? What organizations do you know about that help threatened animals?

Fiction

Authors write **fiction** to tell an imagined story. Every story has these important parts, or elements:

- **Characters**, or the animals or people in the story
- **Setting**, or where and when the story takes place
- **Plot**, or the series of events, conflicts, or obstacles in the story

Authors may make up every aspect of a story. Other times, authors base a story on a real person or place.

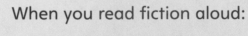 **TURN and TALK** Talk to a partner about how the elements of a fictional story are similar to and different from the elements of an informational text. Take notes on your discussion.

Be a Fluent Reader Reading with fluency requires practice. Fluent readers read with expression. Fiction often contains vivid imagery and precise word choice, which is perfect for practicing expression.

When you read fiction aloud:

- Accent important words and phrases by reading with emphasis.

- Express emotion by making your voice higher- or lower-pitched.

- Change the volume of your voice to match the tone and mood of the story.

TYPES OF FICTION ANCHOR CHART

	Setting	Events	Characters
Realistic	Is or could be a real place	Events could actually happen	Seem real
Historical	Based on a real place and time in the past	Real or made-up events that make sense in the setting	Made up or based on historical figures
Fantasy	Can be a mix of realistic and supernatural or unreal	Fantastic elements often central to the plot	May be unrealistic or imaginary
Science Fiction	Often set in the present or future	Technology often key to the plot	Can include realistic people and imaginary creatures or machines
Mystery	Based on a place in real life, can be historical	Events answer a question or solve a mystery	Realistic but can also be made up or historical

Holling Clancy Holling was born on a Michigan farm in 1900. As a child, he loved raising animals, camping, and drawing. He created remarkable illustrations as early as age 3. As he grew older, he set out to write and illustrate children's books. His unique, detailed drawings help readers dive deeper into his tales of nature and history.

from
Minn of the Mississippi

Preview Vocabulary

As you read *Minn of the Mississippi*, pay attention to these vocabulary words. Notice how they add detail to the story.

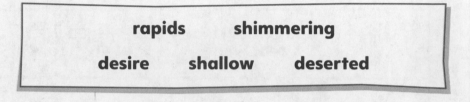

rapids   shimmering

desire   shallow   deserted

Read

Before you begin, establish a purpose for reading. Active readers of fiction follow these strategies when they read a text the first time.

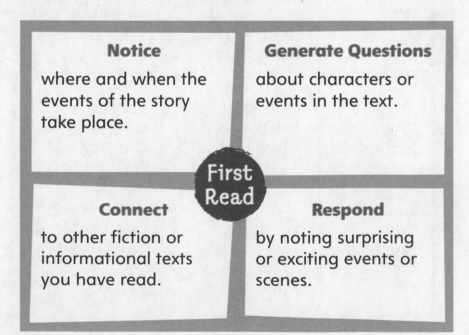

Notice
where and when the events of the story take place.

Generate Questions
about characters or events in the text.

First Read

Connect
to other fiction or informational texts you have read.

Respond
by noting surprising or exciting events or scenes.

from MINN of the MISSISSIPPI

BY HOLLING CLANCY HOLLING

BACKGROUND

This excerpt from a novel follows the adventures of Minn, a young snapping turtle. She travels from the head of the Mississippi River in Minnesota and continues south.

Analyze Plot and Setting

Underline words or phrases that Holling Clancy Holling uses to introduce the plot and setting of the story.

rapids very fast-moving parts of a river

1   Minn the turtle was rather small for this Mississippi! For miles she was a chip caught in rapids and falls. When her tiny rear leg tired, she would drift—until, WHACK! Then she would push away from the boulder, and paddle again. She fought to a shore, a brook and a marsh. After a few weeks of life, Minn felt like a battered old turtle!

MINK

OTTER

2   She came alive when a crawfish tweaked her side. Her angry, baby strike sent her enemy backward. Crows eyed its string of watery mud-clouds puffing along the brook. A raccoon family saw the mud-smoke, and came crawfish hunting. They sat in water, gazing at nothing, feeling under boulders. A sleek otter swirled by like a shadow.

3   Ducks hurtled out of the sky—ripping the surface with spread feet skidding. To Minn they were monsters, hinged at the surface, plunging their heads straight down. They ate bugs and beetles, at times nibbling Minn's rubbery toes with iron-hard beaks. As the air of the wild-rice swamp grew cooler, the sky was fairly a-rustle with leaves and more flying birds. Now spearheads of ducks and long-necked geese flashed by; and a mile up in the clear blue, a ghostly, shimmering ribbon of wild white swans.

4   Flocking crows dotted the trees, cawing, shouting, shrieking, shattering the silence. Some decided to stay on into winter, but not the old crow, whose air-trail southward lay above this marsh. He hated cold! With old cronies he flapped away.

RACCOONS HUNTING FOR CRAWFISH

CLOSE READ

Vocabulary in Context

Context clues are hints found within a sentence, paragraph, or passage that readers can use to determine the meanings of unfamiliar words.

Underline the context clues that help you determine the meaning of *cawing*.

shimmering shining with a soft, flickering light

MUSKRAT

Analyze Plot and Setting

Underline sentences that show how the setting creates conflict during the story's rising action.

desire a powerful wish or longing for something

5   Little Minn felt numb. A cold-blooded reptile, she depended on warmth of air or water to keep her active. Searching in a slow, dull way for something, she spent long moments staring at muddy bottom. She had a desire to dig in it. . . . Deeply. . . .

6   Muskrats towed marsh-roots to their rounded houses. Beavers stored poplar poles for the tasty bark. Otter and mink fished in ice-fringed streams. Big-footed snowshoe rabbits changed their brown coats to white. Pine squirrels flickered like running flames in the trees.

7   Then white flakes laid a pad over the earth to be stitched by everything moving, from mice to moose. New cold came; deeper snow. Life itself appeared to be chilled to an icy stop. Yet chipmunks and bears were only asleep. Frozen flies and mosquitoes were still living. While Minn, long since burrowed deep in the mud, was yet alive. . . .

BEAVER

Use Text Evidence

Highlight evidence that helps you understand how the setting affects events, including Minn's actions.

BREATHING AGAIN!

8   Minn slept through the winter, living on the air stored in her strong lungs. Now, beneath mud and water, she felt new spring warmth. Like a sleep-walker she dug her way out, floated to the surface, and breathed again. But floods hurled dazed Minn through the marsh and into the Mississippi. It was a week before she found a quiet new swamp.

UP FROM THE WINTER SLEEP

9   The food from her food-sac, together with a few beetles and grubs, had carried her through winter hibernation. Now she was thin, weak and hungry! Many a wiggling thing was snapped up to make Minn bigger. Some of her hunting was done by "ambush." Under mud, unseen, her jaws snapped when food came near— and an unlucky snail or worm promptly vanished. Sometimes she hunted by walking along the swamp bottom. Several kinds of turtles are bottom-walkers, though awkward about it. Minn somehow balanced her weight so that enough of it held her down, and her rear-end limp did not matter. Slowly she walked through veils of green water like a River Spirit seeking forgotten things. Among swirling weeds, Minn with her stately, relentless tread was an ancient monster marching out of the past. Two inches of relentless monster. A born hunter.

BOTTOM-WALKING

AMBUSH

CLOSE READ

Analyze Plot and Setting

Underline actions Minn takes that are a direct result of her environment.

Vocabulary in Context

Use context clues to determine the meaning of *upholstered*.

<u>Underline</u> the context clues that support your definition.

shallow not very deep

10   Minn's neighbors, the pert little terrapin, buttoned themselves to logs for hours, basking in the sun. Hot, dry sunlight discourages leeches and mossy growths, so the terrapin's shells were neatly smooth. Minn preferred watery shade to sun—and so leeches became her close company, and tiny plants upholstered her shell in green velvet. This mossy coating would be shed each year. As her shell grew, spreading outward, its top layer would peel off like shreds of snapshot film, leaving her smooth and clean. Minn was deaf—yet felt even faint vibrations. She was shy—but when she looked upon her world she saw clearly, and she knew one color from another. She had much common sense.

11   In high water, Minn had settled in a deep pool of the swamp. When floods ran away, the pool shrank to a shallow pond. The day came when Minn's back bulged above a drying puddle, baking in the sun. Terrapin gulped food in or out of water. But Minn, a snapper, could not swallow easily except under water—and there just wasn't enough water left!

A SNAPPER'S WATER-PIE FOR DINNER

① FISH_____ 34.2%

② CARRION
(DEAD THINGS)_____ 19.6%

③ OTHER VER'-TE-BRATES
(HAVING BACKBONES)_____ 2.2%

④ WATER PLANTS_____ 36.2%

⑤ IN-VER'-TE-BRATES
(WITHOUT BACKBONES,
SUCH AS INSECTS, ETC.)_____ 7.8%

_____

TOTAL PIE   100.0%

(PERCENTAGES FROM DR. KARL F. LAGLER,
"ECONOMIC RELATIONS OF TURTLES")

---

12   Minn had no intention of starving. She splashed through scum to a baked-clay bank, and limped away. Minn on land was different from Minn in water. In a swamp she lived calmly, snapping mainly to capture food. Here, her sensitive eyes disliked bright sun; she felt mean enough to snap at anything. A porcupine met her and she hissed like a viper. The big, bristling rodent backed up as she tottered past. When a fox put down an inquisitive nose, Minn lunged at it. Her shell was less than three inches; but her neck and tail were so long that almost eight inches of angry reptile snaked forward in that strike. Though she missed and fell on her chin, the fox was impressed. When Minn arose again, an armored warrior advancing, the fox switched his plume of a tail from the brush that held it, and thoughtfully trotted off into thick ferns. After all, he *had* eaten well, this morning!

CLOSE READ

Analyze Plot and Setting

Underline a sentence or sentences that show how the setting affects Minn's character.

CLOSE READ

Use Text Evidence

Highlight evidence that supports your understanding of how the setting changes in this passage.

deserted left someone or something alone

Fluency

Read paragraphs 14–16 aloud to a small group. Remember to read with accuracy and at a conversational rate so that your audience understands what you are reading to them.

13   Minn's waddling took her farther away from the Mississippi. In a bubbling brook she ate happily, bottom-walking upstream. But again Minn's water-world deserted her! One day the brook stopped flowing! It gurgled and ran away, while crows fell out of the sky to feast on flopping minnows and tadpoles in the mud.

14   Minn scrambled to safety under draggled grass at the bank. She was confused. First, part of a wide swamp had shrunk to a puddle. Now a running brook had wandered away. Minn stared blankly about her. Then, seeming to get an idea, she started to walk. The gurgling brook had gasped, and then had run away downhill; yet Minn walked up—to a ridge of dead trees, sod and mud making a dam and a pond.

15   Boys who had built the dam in the brook called this place an "Ole Swimmin' Hole." Their fathers just could not understand how a brook, choked with boulders, poles and clay, produced better swimming than clean lakes and beaches of this summer-resort land. The boys could not explain it either—except that—well, how could you feel that a long lake belonged to you? While a dam—built with your own hands—it made a swimmin' hole to be proud of! Even if cows did think they owned the whole thing!

16   Now, dried-out Minn took over. She owned the swimmin' hole! She found the pool to her liking— exactly. But startled boys glimpsed a "Something"—now here, now there—and raced for help. Fathers (and sisters) came to fight this MONSTER!

CLOSE READ

Analyze Plot and Setting

Underline words and phrases that tell you how the plot and setting change.

Develop Vocabulary

In fiction, authors choose words that will help the reader picture what is happening in the text. Precise and descriptive words increase readers' understanding of the story.

My TURN Complete the web of vocabulary words. Write a sentence explaining how each word helps you picture the places in the story.

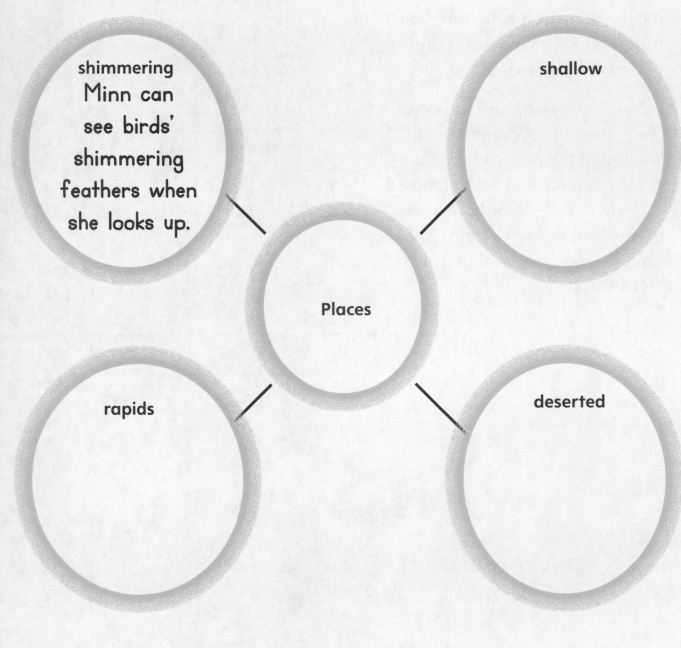

shimmering
Minn can see birds' shimmering feathers when she looks up.

shallow

Places

rapids

deserted

Check for Understanding

My TURN Look back at the text to answer the questions.

1. How do you know that *Minn of the Mississippi* is a fictional text?

2. Why does Holling Clancy Holling include thoughts from other animals instead of only Minn's thoughts?

3. Why does Minn become a monster at the end of the story? Cite text evidence to support your answer.

4. How does Minn change over the course of the story?

Analyze Plot and Setting

In a narrative, the **setting** is where and when a story takes place. The **plot** is the sequence of events, including the rising action, climax, falling action, and resolution. The setting of a story can influence the story's plot.

1. **My TURN** Record what happens at the beginning, middle, and end of *Minn of the Mississippi*. Then go to the Close Read notes in the text and underline parts that show when the plot and setting change.

2. **Text Evidence** Use the parts you underlined to complete the graphic organizer.

Beginning

Plot: Minn starts her life, navigates the stream, and hibernates.

Setting: She is "caught in rapids and falls" of the Mississippi.

Middle

Plot:

Setting:

End

Plot:

Setting:

TURN and TALK Using your completed graphic organizer, discuss with a partner what the plot and setting tell you about Minn. How has she changed during the story?

Use Text Evidence

You can **use text evidence**, or information from the text, to analyze changes in the plot and setting. As you read, mark places where the setting or plot changes. Then use what you marked to analyze the author's choices in the text.

1. **My TURN** Go back to the Close Read notes and highlight evidence that shows the setting influences the story.

2. **Text Evidence** Use your highlighted evidence to complete the chart.

Text Evidence	Why Did the Author Include This Detail?
"Now, beneath mud and water, she felt new spring warmth."	to show the way Minn feels at the end of her hibernation

Analyze your evidence. What conclusion can you draw about how Holling Clancy Holling used setting in this story?

_____

_____

_____

_____

Reflect and Share

Write to Sources In *Minn of the Mississippi*, Minn's environment changes over and over again, causing her to move and find a new place to call home. What other important setting changes have you read about? Use the following process to write and support a response.

Annotating Sources Writers respond to literature to learn how other authors present ideas. When responding to literature, writers choose specific examples from the text to support their responses. To find these examples, writers annotate, or mark up, the text.

To write your response, choose two texts that you enjoyed best or found the most interesting. Use these questions to help you annotate:

- What details describe the setting? Mark the details that stand out to you.
- How does the setting change? Mark where.
- What are the effects of the setting change? Mark details that tell you how the characters are affected.

Review your annotations and use them to write your response. To support your ideas, cite some of the text evidence you annotated.

Weekly Question

What challenges do animals face in their environments?

Academic Vocabulary

Learning Goal

I can develop knowledge about language to make connections between reading and writing.

Context clues are words and phrases that help readers determine the meanings of unfamiliar words. Authors sometimes define an unfamiliar word in or near the sentence that uses the word. They use signal words and punctuation to draw attention to the definition.

 My TURN For each sentence,

1. **Read** the sentence.

2. **Identify** the context clue for the boldfaced academic vocabulary word.

3. **Write** a definition of the word.

Sentence	Type of Context Clue	Definition
It took a few months, but the family **survived**, or lived through, training their first puppy.	comma with a definition after it	Survived means "lived through."
She **classified** her music by genre first and then by artist name.		
As they **acquire** new skills, players get to be experts in the sport.		
The family's food supply was **sufficient** to last for the whole trip.		

Irregular Plurals

Some plural forms of nouns do not end in -s or -es. **Irregular plurals** are nouns that are made plural by changing their spelling. Irregular plurals can also be nouns that have the same singular and plural form, such as the word *moose*, which is spelled the same in both the singular and plural forms.

The word *feet* in paragraph 3 of *Minn of the Mississippi* is an irregular plural noun. The singular of *feet* is *foot*. The spelling of the singular noun *foot* must change to make the plural form *feet*.

My TURN Complete the chart. Use a print or online dictionary to confirm or correct the spelling of each plural noun if needed. Then read each irregular plural noun.

Singular	Plural
deer	
mouse	
tooth	
goose	
sheep	
child	

Read Like a Writer

Authors use **figurative language** to describe characters, setting, and plot. Figurative language includes similes, metaphors, and imagery. A **simile** compares two things using the words *like* or *as*. A **metaphor** compares two things without using comparison words.

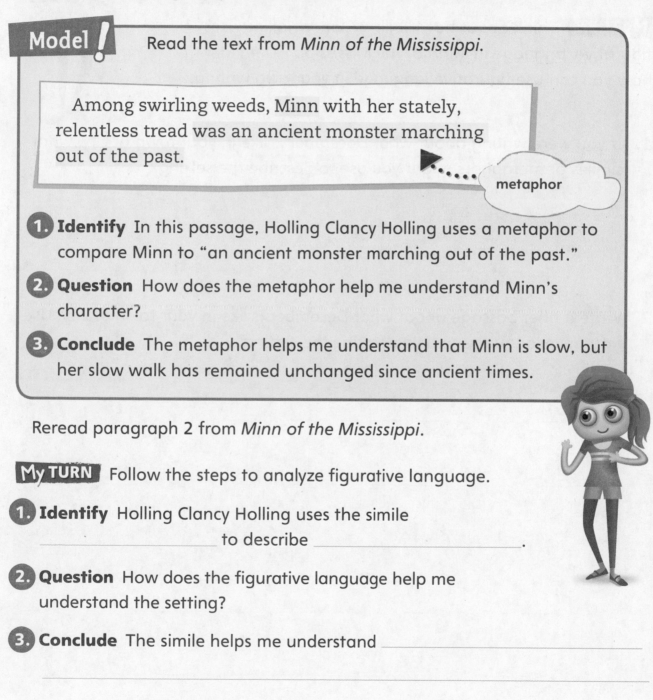

Model Read the text from *Minn of the Mississippi.*

> Among swirling weeds, Minn with her stately, relentless tread was an ancient monster marching out of the past.

metaphor

1. **Identify** In this passage, Holling Clancy Holling uses a metaphor to compare Minn to "an ancient monster marching out of the past."

2. **Question** How does the metaphor help me understand Minn's character?

3. **Conclude** The metaphor helps me understand that Minn is slow, but her slow walk has remained unchanged since ancient times.

Reread paragraph 2 from *Minn of the Mississippi.*

My TURN Follow the steps to analyze figurative language.

1. **Identify** Holling Clancy Holling uses the simile _____ to describe _____ .

2. **Question** How does the figurative language help me understand the setting?

3. **Conclude** The simile helps me understand _____

_____

_____

327

Write for a Reader

Authors use figurative language, such as similes and metaphors, to help readers picture a story's setting, plot, and characters.

Use *like* or *as* to write a simile.

My TURN Think about how Holling Clancy Holling uses figurative language in *Minn of the Mississippi*. Then identify how you can use figurative language in your own writing.

1. If you were writing about what December is like in your town or city, what similes or metaphors might you use to describe the setting?

_____

_____

_____

2. Write a brief passage about what December is like in your town or city. Use figurative language to help describe the setting.

_____

_____

_____

_____

_____

_____

_____

_____

Spell Words with Irregular Plurals

Regular plural nouns are nouns that end in -s or -es. The spelling of these words does not change. **Irregular plural nouns** change the original singular spellings of the words. Irregular plurals can also be nouns that have the same singular and plural form.

My TURN Read the words. Spell and sort the list words by singular and plural forms. Nouns that have the same spelling in their singular and plural forms should be spelled in both columns.

SPELLING WORDS

tooth	teeth	shelf	shelves
halves	leaf	leaves	scissors
veto	vetoes	antenna	antennae
ox	oxen	species	life
lives	moose	echo	echoes

Singular

Plural

Common and Proper Nouns

Common nouns name any person, place, or thing. **Proper nouns** name a specific person, place, or thing. Some proper nouns may contain more than one word. Proper nouns are always capitalized.

Type of Noun	Common Noun	Proper Noun
person	man woman friend author	Pablo Jones Mrs. Tibor Callie Kimberley Jane Pryor
place	school country state street	Jefferson Elementary Mexico Wyoming Main Street
thing	day book club game	Friday *Alice in Wonderland* Weston Drama Club World Series

My TURN Edit this draft to replace the underlined common nouns with proper nouns.

Minn of Mississippi was written by <u>an author</u>. This story is about a turtle named <u>turtle</u>. <u>This turtle</u> spends the first part of her life caught in the <u>river's</u> rapids. Toward the end of the story, <u>the turtle</u> finds a pond called <u>a place</u>. She takes over the spot!

Compose a Headline

To decide what to read in a newspaper, in a magazine, or online, a reader first scans headlines and photographs. A headline must grab the reader's attention. It must also

• be truthful.
• be easy to understand.
• use active, interesting verbs.
• make the reader want to read more.
• be concise, or use as few words as possible.

My TURN Read the article. Then combine words and phrases from the Headline Box to compose a headline that will make a reader want to read more. Write your headline on the line.

_____

   You glimpse the arrow's feathers from the car window. "Stop!" your mom yells. Your dad walks back along the road. He studies an arrowhead drilled into the ground. Is the road under attack? No! Your family just found one of many markers along the Quanah Parker Trail in the Texas Panhandle.

Headline Box

What You Can See	Arrows	Panhandle
Pierce	Plains	Pointed
Along Roads	Finding	Following
Rushing By	Look at This	Trail Marker

My TURN Use this skill when you compose a headline for your travel article.

Compose Body Paragraphs

The first paragraph or two of a travel article is the **lead**, which includes a main idea and draws readers in with short answers to questions of *Who*, *What*, *Where*, *When*, *Why*, and *How*. **Body paragraphs** go beyond the lead to give readers more information.

In a travel article, body paragraphs can be short, but each one should have a topic sentence about an important characteristic of the destination. Each body paragraph should also include details that support the topic sentence. Details may be facts, definitions, concrete details, quotations, or examples.

Writers organize details logically within a paragraph. They may begin with the most important detail and end with the least important detail, or the reverse. Writers may also organize a paragraph using facts in chronological or numerical order. No matter what organization the writer chooses, all the information in the paragraph should relate to the topic sentence.

My TURN The topic sentence is number 1. Number the details to show the order in which they should go to support the topic sentence.

1   There are many places to stay.

_____ Three of the campgrounds have all the modern conveniences.

_____ For travelers on a budget, several motels offer rates under $100 a night.

_____ Expect to pay from $100 to $300 a night at a hotel.

_____ For a small fee, you can park your camper at a county campground.

_____ Options range from fancy hotels to campsites.

My TURN Compose body paragraphs for your travel article in your writing notebook.

Group Paragraphs into Sections

In a travel article, sections should contain paragraphs of related information. **Section headings** help readers find information. Headings should be short, or less than ten words, and specific to the information that will be provided.

My TURN Group the following paragraph topics into sections. Use the chart to list the topics in each section. After you organize a section, write a section heading to name the category into which the topics fit.

Topic Box			
forests water parks	family restaurants bird watching	hiking trails caves	trolley tour balloon ride

	Section Heading 1	Section Heading 2
Paragraph 1 Topic		
Paragraph 2 Topic		
Paragraph 3 Topic		
Paragraph 4 Topic		

My TURN Group paragraphs into sections when you compose a travel article in your writing notebook.

Develop Transitions

Transition words and phrases guide readers from one idea to the next. Writers use transitions to connect sentences or paragraphs and to focus their writing. The chart shows examples of some transitions.

Time	Place	Cause and Effect	Comparison	Contrast	Conclusion
first	above	because	similarly	otherwise	overall
next	below	as a result	likewise	however	in the end
later	nearby	due to	in that way	alternative	to sum up

My TURN Insert a transition on each blank line in the paragraph to lead readers logically from one idea to the next.

Climb to the skydeck _____ the exhibit hall to view the surrounding city. _____ the skydeck wraps around the building, you can see in every direction. _____, climb back down to the exhibit hall. _____ of seeing the city from up high, you can better appreciate the history of how it grew.

My TURN Use transitions to connect sentences and paragraphs as you compose a focused travel article in your writing notebook.

Add a transition whenever a reader might miss the connection between two ideas.

Compose with Multimedia

A **medium** is a way of communicating, such as through written text. The plural of *medium* is *media*. When you include **multimedia** in a text, you communicate in more than one way.

In a travel article, your use of media can include illustrations, such as maps and photographs. If you publish your article online, you can also use video, sound, and animation.

My TURN Which media would work best in your travel article? Explain how each medium you check would help an audience understand the article's main idea. Share your chart with your Writing Club.

Medium	Use It?	Why?
Illustrations	☐	
Photographs	☐	
Video	☐	
Sound	☐	
Animation	☐	

My TURN Identify a topic, purpose, and audience. Then select any genre, and plan a draft by mapping your ideas.

INTERACTIVITY

Part of a
HABITAT

A butterfly egg is laid on a plant. After several days, a caterpillar comes out of the egg and begins to feed on the plant.

The adult butterfly comes out of the chrysalis. Soon, it will fly away and search for food.

The caterpillar continues to eat and grow.

Weekly Question

In what ways do living things depend on each other?

Quick Write How does a caterpillar depend on a leaf? How does a toad or a bird depend on a caterpillar? Take notes about how animals depend on each other to survive.

The fully grown caterpillar sheds its skin and begins to turn into a chrysalis. Inside the chrysalis, an amazing transformation takes place.

Learning Goal

I can learn more about poetry by analyzing poetic language and elements.

Poetry is usually read aloud. This helps the reader listen for rhythm and rhyme.

Poetry

Poetry is a form of writing that focuses on the arrangement of words to express ideas or feelings. Elements of poetry include

- **Structure,** or the arrangement of lines or groups of lines (called **stanzas**)
- **Rhythm,** or the pattern of words, created by the arrangement of stressed and unstressed syllables (called **meter**)
- **Rhyme,** or two or more words with the same ending sounds
- **Figurative language,** or words with meanings beyond their everyday definitions

Establish Purpose One purpose for reading poetry is to enjoy its precise use of language. As you read the selection, notice how the informational text that accompanies the poetry answers the question in the poem.

TURN and TALK In a small group, discuss how a poem can have a similar purpose to an informational text. Identify how the characteristics of each genre are different. Then set your purpose for reading.

My PURPOSE _____

_____

_____

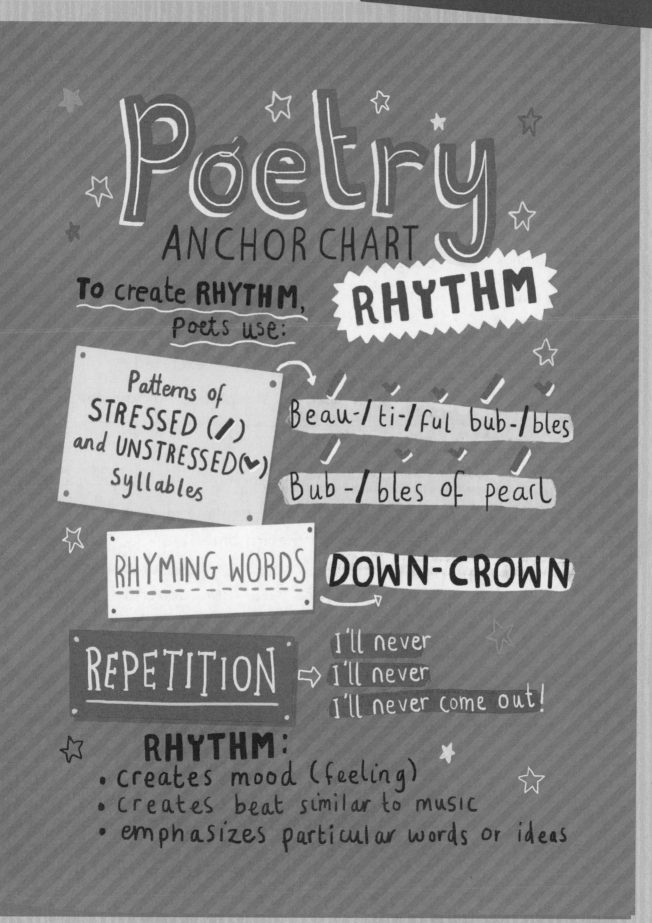

Poetry
ANCHOR CHART

RHYTHM

To create **RHYTHM,**
Poets use:

Patterns of
STRESSED (/)
and **UNSTRESSED (˅)**
Syllables

Beau-/ti-/ful bub-/bles

Bub-/bles of pearl

RHYMING WORDS   **DOWN-CROWN**

REPETITION ⇒
I'll never
I'll never
I'll never come out!

RHYTHM:
- creates mood (feeling)
- creates beat similar to music
- emphasizes particular words or ideas

Joyce Sidman is an award-winning children's writer and poet. At home in Minnesota, she enjoys taking walks and absorbing the natural world around her. Many of the details she notices end up in her writing. She loves poetry because it is "so vivid and sleek—like a race car. No extra words."

from

Butterfly Eyes and Other Secrets of the Meadow

Preview Vocabulary

As you read the selections from *Butterfly Eyes and Other Secrets of the Meadow*, pay attention to these vocabulary words. Notice how they relate to the information in the poems.

tender	excreted
vessels	steeped	ultraviolet

Read

Active readers of **poetry** follow these strategies when they read a text the first time.

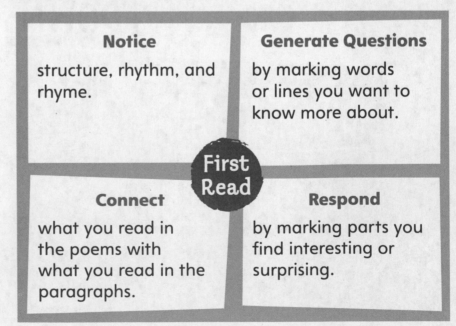

Notice structure, rhythm, and rhyme.

Generate Questions by marking words or lines you want to know more about.

First Read

Connect what you read in the poems with what you read in the paragraphs.

Respond by marking parts you find interesting or surprising.

from Butterfly Eyes
and Other Secrets
of the
Meadow

by JOYCE SIDMAN

illustrated by
BETH KROMMES

BACKGROUND

Poetry and prose are combined in the following
selection to explore different parts of life in
a meadow. Each pair of poems focuses on a
meadow insect or animal and the plant that
it relies on, introducing important elements
of the relationship. The prose explains the
relationship in more detail.

🔊 AUDIO

✏️ ANNOTATE

Explain Poetic Language and Elements

Repetition draws a reader's attention and adds emphasis to a topic. <u>Underline</u> the repeated related words that make up the central image of this poem.

tender soft or gentle; easily damaged

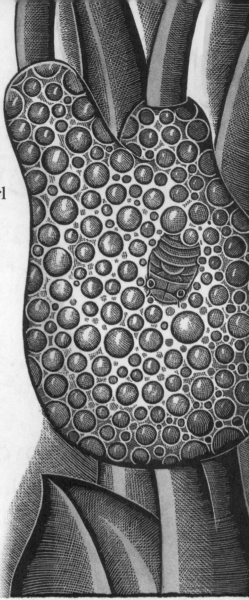

Bubble Song

Beautiful bubbles
bubbles of pearl,
all in a clustery, bubbly swirl
Bubbles I blow
5 from my own bubble-spout
(I'll never
    I'll never
        I'll never come out!)

Beautiful bubbles
10 bubbles of foam
Bubbly castle,
snug bubble-home
keeps my skin tender
saves me from drought
15 (I'll never
    I'll never
        I'll never come out!)

Beautiful bubbles
bubbles of spume
20 guard me and hide me
in my bubble-room
Until I'm a grownup
and wings fully sprout
I'll never
25   I'll never
        I'll never come out!

What am I?

Sap Song

I go up

        I go down

from the roots

        to the crown

5   Like a twin

        set of tubes

fetching water

        and food

In each stem

10   that you see

there's a little

        of me

Up and down

        like an ant

15   I'm the veins

        of the plant

What am I?

CLOSE READ

Explain Poetic Language and Elements

Sounds that repeat in a predictable pattern create rhythm and rhyme. Underline the pairs of words that rhyme. One pair, *tubes* and *food*, is similar, but not an exact rhyme.

Visualize Imagery

Highlight information that combines with repeated words in "Bubble Song" to help you form a mental image.

excreted separated and removed from the body

1   Have you ever seen a small glob of foam on a meadow plant? Inside that glob you'll find a 1/8-inch-long spittlebug, the nymph (young) form of an insect also called a froghopper. When spittlebugs hatch from eggs, they latch on to stems and suck sap from the plant. In the spittlebug's body, this sap is mixed with chemicals, then excreted and blown into a froth with a special nozzle on the tip of their abdomens. Until midsummer, when the spittlebug matures into an adult froghopper, it snuggles in its bubbly home, protected from predators, parasites, heat, and the strong summer sun.

2   Spittlebugs suck primarily xylem sap—the sap that comes up from a plant's roots. The xylem and phloem vessels are like the "veins" of a plant, carrying nutrients back and forth and helping to support the stem. Xylem tubes carry water and minerals upward. Phloem tubes carry the sugary food made by the leaves to all parts of the plant.

CLOSE READ

Visualize Imagery

Highlight the phrase that helps you picture the parts of the plant that Joyce Sidman describes in the rhyming lines of "Sap Song."

vessels tubes or passageways carrying fluid around an organism; containers

CLOSE READ

Explain Poetic Language and Elements

A metaphor compares two things without using *like* or *as*. <u>Underline</u> two metaphors in this poem.

steeped soaked; drenched

Heavenly

My pods are famous, of course:
soft green purses
on slim racks.

And my leaves: monarchs
5   adore them.

They plant their babies
and just fly away!

But have you ever
seen me bloom?
10   At high noon

on a midsummer's day
when the pavement is steeped in heat
and cicadas are screaming,
follow my heady perfume
15   and you will track me down:

see my
heavenly
           lavender
                     muffins
20   baking in the sun.

What am I?

346

Ultraviolet

the eyes of these flies
see more than we see
they love scarlet
adore pink
5   thrive on orange
lap up yellow with
long curled tongues
but their favorite
extra-special secret
10   color sprinkled on
tiny wingscales
like valentines
and painted on the
most delectable blossoms
15   like bull's-eyes
that we can't see
because our eyes
are not theirs
is *ultraviolet*

What are they?

CLOSE READ

Explain Poetic Language and Elements

A simile compares two unlike things using the words *like* or *as*. It calls attention to the qualities of one or both things being compared.

Underline two similes in this poem.

ultraviolet related to a color that is invisible to the human eye

Context clues are words and phrases that can be used to define unfamiliar words in a text.

Underline context clues that help you define the word *toxic*.

MILKWEED AND BUTTERFLIES

1   Milkweed is best known for its fluff-filled seedpods, but it is actually named for its milky sap, which is toxic to most insects and animals. Monarch butterflies are immune to these toxins and lay their eggs on the plant's leaves, which provide food for newly hatched caterpillars. By munching on milkweed, Monarch caterpillars (and later, butterflies) become bitter-tasting and even poisonous to most predators, which have learned to avoid them.

2   Butterflies serve a vital role as pollinators of meadow flowers. To attract them, flowers such as daisies and coneflowers are colored with eye-catching ultraviolet patterns that surround their pollen-filled centers. We can't see these patterns, but butterflies can: they have one of the widest ranges of color vision in the animal world. For them, ultraviolet colors—which also show up on their wings and help them identify each other —are like a secret language.

CLOSE READ

Visualize Imagery

Highlight evidence that combines with the similes in "Ultraviolet" to help you picture the world as a butterfly might see it.

Explain Poetic Language and Elements

<u>Underline</u> the lines that contain four syllables and share a rhythmic pattern.

The Gray Ones

We are the tall ones with crowns of velvet
    the high-steppers
    the flag-wavers
We are the silent ones that browse at dusk
5   the bud-nibblers
    the ear-flickers
The gray ones that linger at woods' edge
    Swift   Still
    Here   Gone
10 Eyes of glass
Hooves of stone

We are the ghosts
    of those
    who have come before
15 The gray ones
    Leaping
        Gone

What are we?

We Are Waiting
(a pantoum)

Our time will come again,
say the patient ones.
Now is meadow,
but not for long.

5   Say the patient ones:
sunlight dazzles,
but not for long.
Seedlings grow amongst the grass.

Sunlight dazzles
10   and the meadow voles dance,
but seedlings grow amongst the grass.
Forest will return.

Meadow voles dance
where once was fire,
15   but forest will return.
We wait patiently.

Once was fire.
Now is meadow.
We wait patiently.
20   Our time will come again.

What are we?

CLOSE READ

Explain Poetic Language and Elements

A *pantoum* features stanzas with four lines. Lines are repeated throughout the poem according to a set pattern.

Underline the pair of repeated lines in the first two stanzas.

351

CLOSE READ

Visualize Imagery

Highlight a detail that combines with line 5 in "The Gray Ones" to help the reader create a mental image.

DEER AND TREES

1   Meadows are formed in many different ways. Sometimes a forest burns, is blown down, or is cleared for lumber, leaving open areas. Sometimes a pond or wetland dries out. Meadow plants move in and thrive in these open areas. Then come animals such as the white-tailed deer, which feast on new shoots, shrubs, and berries, but can fade back into the forest at any sign of danger.

2   The land is always changing, however. Tree seedlings take root in the meadow, and the slow march toward forest begins again. This constant change in habitat is called succession.

Develop Vocabulary

Poets use precise language to create images in readers' minds. They carefully choose words that best match what they intend to say. These specific words help readers visualize descriptions and understand a poem's meaning.

My TURN Review the vocabulary word in each circle. For each vocabulary word, write four related words, such as synonyms or phrases with similar meanings. Then, with a partner, discuss which words would create the best images and descriptions in a poem.

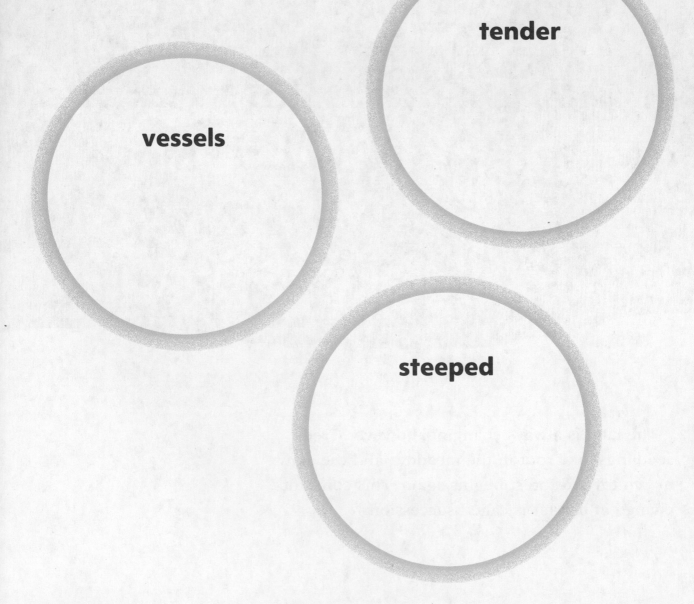

Check for Understanding

My TURN Look back at the text to answer the questions.

1. What genre clues help you distinguish between the poems and prose in *Butterfly Eyes and Other Secrets of the Meadow*?

2. How does Joyce Sidman's choice of structure for the poem "Sap Song" connect to its ideas?

3. Draw a conclusion about who "the patient ones" are in the poem "We Are Waiting." Support your conclusion with text evidence.

4. Analyze the relationships between creatures and plants that are discussed in the text. What do they have in common?

Explain Poetic Language and Elements

Joyce Sidman's poetry expresses emotions and also informs readers. To enjoy and explain poetry, readers notice poetic elements such as **structure, rhythm, meter, figurative language,** and **sound devices**. Sound devices include **rhyme** as well as **assonance** (repetition of the same vowel sounds) and **alliteration** (repetition of the same initial consonant sounds).

1. **MyTURN** Go to the Close Read notes in *Butterfly Eyes and Other Secrets of the Meadow* and underline the parts that help you explain how Joyce Sidman uses poetic elements.

2. **Text Evidence** Use your evidence to complete the chart.

Poem	Evidence	How Elements Create Effects
"Bubble Song" and "Sap Song"	A form of "bubble" is repeated 13 times in "Bubble Song."	Repetition of "bubble" words make an image of an insect home.
"Heavenly" and "Ultraviolet"		
"The Gray Ones" and "We Are Waiting"		

Visualize Imagery

Consider the precise language Joyce Sidman uses to describe plants, animals, and insects in the text. Use these descriptions to visualize, or create mental images of, what she describes.

1. **My TURN** Go back to the Close Read notes and highlight evidence that helps you create mental images.

2. **Text Evidence** Use your highlighted text to describe what you visualized while reading the poems and prose.

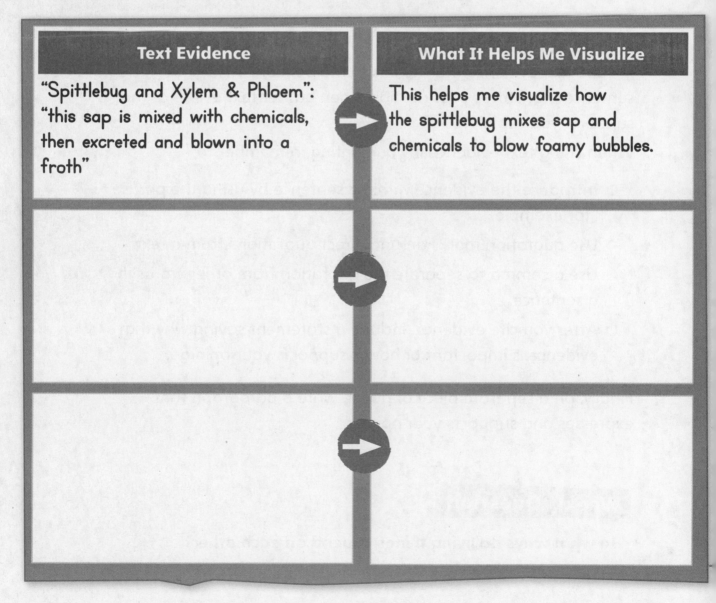

Text Evidence		What It Helps Me Visualize
"Spittlebug and Xylem & Phloem": "this sap is mixed with chemicals, then excreted and blown into a froth"	→	This helps me visualize how the spittlebug mixes sap and chemicals to blow foamy bubbles.
	→	
	→	

Reflect and Share

Write to Sources This week you read about living things that depend on each other. What other living things did you read about this week? What other creatures or plants do they depend on? Choose a pair of animals or plants that are closely related. Then gather text evidence to write an opinion paragraph about the question: Is it important to know how living things depend on one another?

Use Text Evidence In opinion writing, it is important to include text evidence that relates to the opinion. Write one sentence that states your opinion. Then gather text evidence that supports your opinion.

When citing text evidence in your writing, remember to:

- Introduce the evidence within a sentence by using the phrase "for example."
- Use quotation marks around direct quotations from a text.
- Use a comma to separate the quotation from other words in a sentence.
- After you cite evidence, include a statement saying why that evidence is important or how it supports your opinion.

Finally, on a separate piece of paper, write a paragraph that expresses and supports your opinion.

Weekly Question

In what ways do living things depend on each other?

Academic Vocabulary

Analogies compare two things that have something in common. Through analogies, readers expand their vocabulary and make connections between words.

My TURN   For each analogy,

 Identify the relationship between the words in the analogy.

 Write the missing word on the line.

3. Explain the comparison in the analogy.

Water is to **survive** as *pencil* is to _____.

_____

_____

Defense is to *protect* as _____ is to *attack*.

_____

_____

Scientist is to **classifies** as _____ is to *grades*.

_____

_____

Acquire is to *obtain* as *promote* is to _____.

_____

_____

Sufficient is to *adjective*, as *suffice* is to _____.

_____

_____

Greek Roots

Knowing the origin of words and word parts can help you define unfamiliar words. For example, some English words include **Greek roots**, such as *bio*, *phon*, *scope*, *graph*, *meter*, and *tele*. The Greek root *bio* means "life." If you know the Greek root *bio*, you can identify and define words with this root, such as *biology*, which means "the study of life."

My TURN Complete the chart by writing a word that contains each root and a sentence that includes each word.

Greek Root	Root Meaning	Word	Sentence
bio	life	biology	After reading about insects and animal life, I want to learn more about meadow biology.
phon	sound		
scope	looking at		
graph	written or drawn		
meter	measure		
tele	far or distant		

Read Like a Writer

Poets use **imagery** to create an image, or mental picture, of how something looks, sounds, smells, tastes, or feels. Imagery can be developed using figurative language such as **similes** and **metaphors.** Imagery can help readers experience emotions, make connections, and understand ideas.

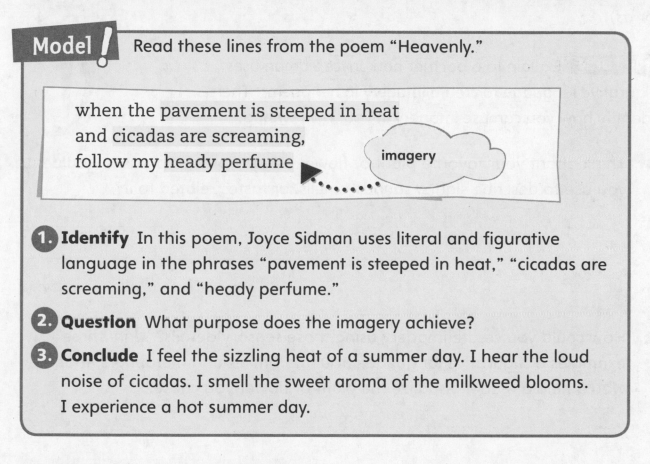

Model ! Read these lines from the poem "Heavenly."

> when the pavement is steeped in heat
> and cicadas are screaming,
> follow my heady perfume ▶ · · · · ·   imagery

1. **Identify** In this poem, Joyce Sidman uses literal and figurative language in the phrases "pavement is steeped in heat," "cicadas are screaming," and "heady perfume."

2. **Question** What purpose does the imagery achieve?

3. **Conclude** I feel the sizzling heat of a summer day. I hear the loud noise of cicadas. I smell the sweet aroma of the milkweed blooms. I experience a hot summer day.

Reread the poem "The Gray Ones."

My TURN Follow the steps to analyze the effects of imagery.

1. **Identify** Joyce Sidman uses imagery in the lines _____

_____

2. **Question** What does the imagery help me see?

3. **Conclude** I see _____

_____

Write for a Reader

Use figurative language to vividly describe how things look, smell, sound, taste, or feel.

Poets and authors use figurative language to help readers create mental pictures. Writers can do this by using metaphors (comparisons that say something is something else) or similes (comparisons that use *like* or *as*).

My TURN Explain to a partner how Joyce Sidman uses figurative language to create imagery in her poems. Then identify how you can use imagery in your own writing.

1. Think about your favorite plant or flower. What words or phrases would you use to describe sights, sounds, smells, or tastes related to it?

_____

_____

_____

2. How could you create imagery using those sensory details? Write three examples of figurative language, including similes and metaphors, that would help a reader visualize the plant or flower you chose.

_____

_____

_____

3. Explain how you would use each figure of speech in a poem to have an effect on your audience. How would your imagery help readers feel as if they are experiencing your plant or flower?

_____

_____

_____

Spell Words with Greek Roots

Knowing the **Greek roots** *bio*, *phon*, *scope*, *graph*, *meter*, and *tele* can help you spell English words with these roots. For example, if you recognize and know how to spell the Greek root *phon*, then it will help you correctly spell words with this root, such as the word *headphones*.

My TURN Read the words. Then spell and alphabetize them. Be sure to spell each Greek root correctly.

SPELLING WORDS

biography	biology	biologist	biome
telephone	microphone	headphones	gyroscope
telescope	periscope	telegraph	pictograph
photograph	kilometer	barometer	centimeter
diameter	teleport	phonics	perimeter

Singular and Plural Nouns

Singular nouns name one person, place, thing, or idea. **Plural nouns** name more than one person, place, or thing and can be formed in different ways. Some plural nouns are formed by adding -s or -es. For some nouns ending in y, the y is replaced with i when the noun changes from the singular to plural form. Other plural nouns use a different spelling from the singular form. For example, the singular noun *woman* changes to *women* in the plural form. Follow these rules when you edit drafts.

Singular Nouns	Plural Nouns	Sentences
man, canoe	men, canoes	The **man** built himself a **canoe**. Two **men** are paddling their **canoes**.
woods, berry	woods, berries	I ate a **berry** while I walked in the **woods**. A bear wandered through the **woods** looking for **berries** to eat.
caterpillar, butterfly	caterpillars, butterflies	A **caterpillar** turns into a **butterfly**. Monarch **butterflies** and **caterpillars** eat milkweed.

My TURN Edit this draft to make sure the correct singular or plural form of the noun is used in each sentence.

> Butterfly play an important part as pollinator of flowers. The flowers have pattern that surround their center. Butterflies can see these pattern, but people cannot. For butterfly, the colors are like a secret code.

My TURN When you edit your writing, make sure to use and spell plural nouns correctly.

Use Linking Words and Phrases

Learning Goal

I can use elements of informational text to write an article.

Writers use transitions, or linking words and phrases, to connect ideas in a paragraph.

Paragraph Topic: Museums

Sentence Topic	Sentence with Linking Word or Phrase
Choice of museums	Families can choose from many memorable museum experiences.
Science museum	**For example,** the science museum has an exhibit on how to build robots.
Art museum	**Another** great stop for kids is the weekly hands-on sculpture workshop.

My TURN Add linking words and phrases to connect the ideas in a paragraph from a travel article about Washington, D.C.

Paragraph Topic: Eating Lunch in the Capital

Sentence Topic	Sentence with Linking Word or Phrase
Lunch	In Washington, D.C., lunch is the main meal of the day.
What it includes	_____ of this, the meal includes protein, such as fish or meat, plus vegetables, salad, and fruit.
Where to buy lunch	_____, at large family restaurants you can order a full lunch and have leftovers for later.

My TURN Add linking words and phrases as you develop the draft of a travel article in your writing notebook.

365

Use Precise Language and Vocabulary

Writers use precise language to give exact information to readers.

Not Precise/Approximate	Precise
It is **kind of far** to walk.	It is **1.5 miles** away.
We will see you **next week**.	We will meet **on Monday**.

Writers use specific vocabulary in order to be precise about a topic.

Not Precise	Precise
Take the **boat** to Staten Island.	Take the **ferry** to Staten Island.

The word *ferry* describes a specific kind of boat that transports people.

My TURN Complete the paragraph with precise language from the Word Bank.

Word Bank

bayou   **brackish**   **concrete**   **waterway's**

A _____ is a very slow-moving creek. In Houston, the bayou has sides paved in _____. In the wild, the same _____ banks are muddy and mucky. Because Houston's bayous are near the ocean, their water is often _____, or salty.

My TURN Use precise language and vocabulary as you develop the draft of a travel article in your writing notebook.

Edit for Capitalization

Writers use these rules of capitalization. Writers use capitalization to signal readers that a name or topic is important.

Category	Rule	Examples
History	Capitalize the main words in names of historical periods, events, and documents.	the Middle Ages the Battle of Bunker Hill the Declaration of Independence
Titles	Capitalize the main words in the titles of books, stories, and essays.	*Little House in the Big Woods* "Hansel and Gretel" "How to Build a Birdhouse"
Languages	Capitalize the names of languages.	Chinese English
People	Capitalize the names of races and nationalities.	Caucasian Apache Venezuelan

My TURN Highlight each letter that should be capitalized.

Cabot Yerxa built a house, by hand, in the style used by hopi Indians. Before that, he ran stores in Alaska and Cuba and served in world war I. Learn more about him in the book *Cabot Yerxa: adventurer*.

My TURN Apply these capitalization rules when you edit the draft of a travel article in your writing notebook.

Capitalize the names of nationalities when you discuss types of food in a travel article.

367

Edit for Adverbs

The **relative adverbs** *where*, *when*, and *why* connect **two related clauses**.

> *Where* is about place: **I found the tickets** *where* **Cindy left them.**
> *When* is about time: **You will return to Paris** *when* **you are ready to fly home.**
> *Why* is about a reason: **He told me** *why* **the park was closed.**

Adverbs of frequency, such as *often* and *never*, describe a **verb** by telling how often it happens.

> I *always* **take** the train.
> *Sometimes* visitors **stay** an extra day.

Adverbs of degree, such as *very*, *highly*, and *slightly*, describe an **adjective** or another **adverb** by telling how strongly it applies to a situation.

> You must be *quite* **athletic** to complete this hike.
> The guide read the words *very* **slowly**.

Often adverbs are words that modify a verb and end in *ly*, such as *quietly* in the following sentence: The students **talked quietly** during free time.

My TURN Edit this paragraph to correct five adverb errors. Cross out the incorrect adverb and write the correct one above it.

> In England, you will never see many flags in one place. These
>
> flags should quite be displayed in a sometimes respectful way.
>
> The most slightly honored flag, called the Royal Standard, only
>
> flies over a British castle why the ruler is there.

My TURN Edit for adverbs when you revise the draft of a travel article in your writing notebook.

Edit for Coordinating Conjunctions

Writers use the three **coordinating conjunctions**—*and*, *but*, and *or*.

Writers use **and** to combine subjects or predicates. The **subject** of a sentence is a **noun** or a **pronoun**. The **predicate** of a sentence is a **verb**.

People **drive** cars.

- If two sentences have the same verb, combine them into one sentence with a **compound subject**:

   Trains **and** buses **run** between the cities.

- If two sentences have the same subject, combine them into one sentence with a **compound predicate**:

   Planes **take off and land** every 30 seconds.

Writers use a comma plus **and, but**, and **or** to combine whole related sentences. This makes a **compound sentence**. Each conjunction does its own job.

- **And** adds information:

   The Capitol is where lawmakers meet, **and** it bustles with activity.

- **But** shows a difference:

   It can be nice at the National Mall, **but** it quickly gets muddy in the rain.

- **Or** shows a choice:

   Show your ticket, **or** wait in the line over there.

My TURN Rewrite each pair of sentences into a single sentence.

1. The dolphins put on a show. The killer whales put on a show.

   _____

2. The sailors undid the ropes. The sailors pushed the boat from the dock.

   _____

My TURN Use coordinating conjunctions when you edit the draft of a travel article in your writing notebook.

INTERACTIVITY

Many Ways to Be
ONE OF A KIND

Animals use their adaptations to get food and stay safe. These adaptations show how each animal is different in its own special way.

These finches are a famous example of the way animal bodies change in response to the environment. The birds are closely related to each other but have very different beak shapes. Each beak shape is suited to finding a particular kind of food.

Beak

Tongue
Groove

Beak

Lamellae

The hummingbird's unusual beak has been compared to a straw, a sponge, and even a pump. Recent scientific studies revealed that the hummingbird's thin tongue parts as it brings nectar into the bird's mouth.

Weekly Question

How do adaptations make animals unique?

Rattlesnakes grow specially shaped scales at the ends of their tails. A section of the rattle is added every time the snake sheds its skin. To scare off predators, rattlesnakes shake their tails rapidly, causing the special scales to clatter against each other.

Illustrate Draw an animal that has adapted to its environment. On a separate sheet of paper, write a paragraph to explain how the adaptation makes the animal unique.

A spider's web is strong, lightweight, and flexible. The material of the web, sometimes called "silk," starts as a liquid inside special parts of the spider's body, called spinnerets. As it moves through the spinnerets, the liquid becomes a solid thread.

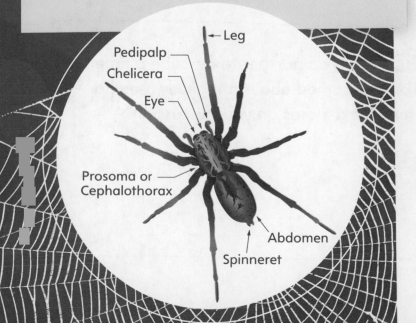

Leg
Pedipalp
Chelicera
Eye
Prosoma or Cephalothorax
Abdomen
Spinneret

371

Spotlight on Genre

Informational Text

Informational texts come in many forms. You know about autobiography, biography, and magazine articles. Other forms include

Newspapers

- Newspapers are published more frequently than magazines.
- Newspaper articles report facts in a timely fashion.
- They focus on keeping people informed about recent events.

Reference books

- Reference books are not updated frequently and contain information that does not change quickly.
- You can learn word meanings, pronunciations, and different forms of a word from a dictionary.
- Some dictionaries also tell you about a word's roots and history.
- An encyclopedia contains a collection of short, factual entries.
- Each entry is about a single topic.

How can I gain deeper understanding of a topic?

TURNandTALK Ask a partner to describe a time when he or she learned about a topic by reading multiple texts. Take notes on your discussion.

My NOTES _____

_____

_____

Informational Text Anchor Chart

Purpose = inform or explain

Features Real world
One main idea
Factual key details
Possible text features

Features of Texts

- Current events
- Historical newspapers for historical events

- Brief, compact
- Factual information

- Current
- In-depth REPORTING on issues

- Definitions
- Pronunciations
- Parts of speech

DICTIONARY

Mike Jung is the author of two books for kids, *Geeks, Girls, and Secret Identities* and *Unidentified Suburban Object*. He loves reading about animals, especially weird animals, so he was thrilled to write about echidnas!

The Weird and Wonderful Echidna

Preview Vocabulary

As you read *The Weird and Wonderful Echidna*, pay attention to these vocabulary words. Think about how they may convey specific information about the topic shared by both texts.

> unique   monotremes
>
> adaptations   burrow

Read

Before you begin, establish a purpose for reading. Readers of **informational text** follow these strategies when they read a text the first time.

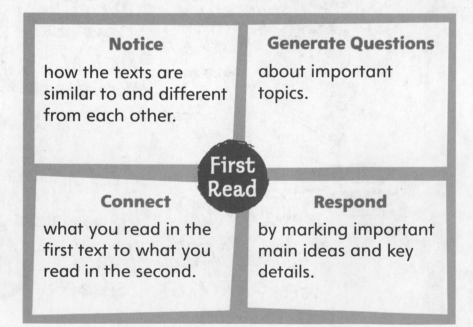

Notice

how the texts are similar to and different from each other.

Generate Questions

about important topics.

First Read

Connect

what you read in the first text to what you read in the second.

Respond

by marking important main ideas and key details.

The **Weird** and **Wonderful** Echidna

by Mike Jung

AUDIO

ANNOTATE

Monitor Comprehension

Highlight evidence that you would include in a mental summary to clarify your understanding.

unique unusual; unlike anything else

monotremes animals that are mammals but lay eggs

adaptations changes that make a plant or animal better suited to an environment

1   Australia is home to some of the most unique animals on Earth. Kangaroos and koalas live here. A giant bird called the emu does, too. Of all the creatures that live in Australia, the echidna is one of the strangest. This small creature makes its home in Australia and also on the island of New Guinea.

2   The echidna is also known by its common name, the spiny anteater. The name describes two of the echidna's amazing traits. All echidnas have spines. Some eat ants. But those are only two of the traits of this strange and wonderful creature.

3   If you met an echidna, you might have a hard time figuring out what kind of animal it is. To begin with, the echidna has a beak. But it doesn't have feathers and it doesn't fly, so it's not a bird. The echidna lays soft eggs like a snake does, but the echidna is not a reptile. The echidna is a mammal.

4   The echidna belongs to a group of mammals known as monotremes. They are the only mammals on Earth that lay eggs. There are only two kinds of monotremes. One is the echidna, and the other is the platypus. Monotremes have lived on Earth longer than any other mammals. Several adaptations have helped them to thrive.

Short-billed echidna

The one species of short-beaked echidna lives throughout Australia and on New Guinea.

5   The echidna's beak is a rare feature among mammals. It's also a fabulously adapted tool for finding food. Echidnas live in forested areas and feed on insects, worms, and other tiny creatures.

6   An echidna's beak is long and pointy. However, the beak doesn't have two halves that open, like a bird's beak. Instead, the echidna uses its beak as a digging tool. It pokes and prods to find its prey. The echidna's beak is tough. In fact, it's strong enough to break open a rotten log or dig into the soil in search of a tasty meal.

7   The most amazing thing about the echidna's beak is something you can't see. The beak has sensors inside it. The sensors detect electrical signals given off by living creatures. That means an echidna can locate prey without seeing, hearing, or touching it. It's a kind of mammal superpower!

The three species of long-beaked echidna are found exclusively on the island of New Guinea.

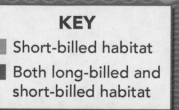

New Guinea

Indian Ocean

Pacific Ocean

Australia

Long-billed echidna

KEY
- Short-billed habitat
- Both long-billed and short-billed habitat

CLOSE READ

Synthesize Information

<u>Underline</u> facts that give important information about how the echidna finds prey.

Monitor Comprehension

Highlight details that combine with your background knowledge to improve your comprehension.

8   An echidna's mouth is small, and it has no teeth. The echidna uses its beak to crush a worm or insect into tiny pieces. Then it takes the pieces into its mouth and swallows them.

9   Scientists classify echidnas according to beak length. There are short-beaked echidnas and long-beaked echidnas. The one species of short-beaked echidna lives throughout Australia and on New Guinea. The three species of long-beaked echidna are found exclusively on the island of New Guinea.

10   If you were to see an echidna in person, the first thing you might notice is its coat of spines. The spines are short and hollow. They are made of keratin, the same material that makes up your hair and fingernails.

The colors of an echidna's fur and spines help it blend into its surroundings.

Can you find me?

11   An echidna's spines are like a coat of armor. They protect the echidna from predators such as the dingo, a kind of wild dog. When a predator approaches, an echidna rolls itself up into a ball. The ball appears to be nothing *but* spines. Predators usually think twice before chomping down.

12   In addition, the echidna's spines play another important role. They serve as camouflage to help the animal hide from predators. The spines are colored with sections of white, black, and brown. The spines blend well with the surrounding colors of rocks, soil, and dead leaves.

13   Like all other mammals, the echidna also has fur, though some echidnas are furrier than others. The amount of fur depends upon where the echidnas live. Echidnas occupy a range of habitats, from the chillier regions of Australia to warmer, drier places in New Guinea. The ones in colder areas tend to have more fur. Those in warmer climates have less.

Monitor Comprehension
Highlight facts that can help you monitor your comprehension by checking for visual cues.

OUCH!

The strong, sharp spines of an echidna help keep it safe from predators.

What's for dinner?

The echidna has many features, like its long tongue, that are adapted to meet its needs.

Synthesize Information

Underline text that supports an idea from paragraph 2.

14   If you think the echidna's beak and spines are incredible, wait until you see its tongue! The echidna's tongue is a simply amazing tool. And it's perfectly adapted to capture the kinds of prey the echidna needs.

15   There are two different kinds of echidna tongues. That's because different kinds of echidnas eat different kinds of food. One type of echidna has a long sticky tongue; the other type has a short tongue that is covered with hooks.

16   It may seem backward, but the short-beaked echidna has a long, sticky tongue. The tongue is extremely flexible. It's great for grabbing ants, termites, and other tiny prey. The short-beaked echidna is expert at flicking its tongue into the nooks and crannies where those animals live.

17   The long-beaked echidna doesn't eat ants at all. In fact, worms are its only prey. But its tongue is perfectly adapted for worm catching. The long-beaked echidna probes the soil with its beak. When it finds a worm, it sticks out its tongue. The tiny hooks on the tongue hook into the earthworm. Then the echidna pulls its tongue back into its mouth, and the earthworm becomes lunch!

18   When it comes to predators, the echidna has another secret weapon: its claws. When an echidna is startled or attacked, it hides by doing something no other mammal in the world can do. It digs itself straight down into the ground.

19   How does the echidna pull off this trick? The claws play a big role. Tough and heavy, they can move a lot of dirt in a short amount of time. Other adaptations help the claws do their job.

20   First of all, the echidna has a strong skeleton. Second, the echidna might be small, but it's incredibly muscular. Those muscles can pull hard to dig very fast!

21   When a predator approaches, the claws, skeleton, and muscles of the echidna go to work. In seconds, the small mammal can burrow almost completely into the earth! Once the echidna is dug in, its camouflage spines make it very hard to see. And because the only part that's exposed is spines, many predators will pass it by.

CLOSE READ

Monitor Comprehension

Lists of facts can be difficult to understand on first reading. Highlight text that signals a good place to pause and check your understanding.

burrow dig a hole

Vocabulary in Context

Use **context clues,** such as examples and categories, to determine the meanings of unfamiliar terms.

Define *dingo*. Use a dictionary to confirm your definition. <u>Underline</u> the category to which a dingo belongs.

22   What's the echidna's most amazing adaptation? Some people might think it is the beak. Others might vote for the spines or the echidna's digging ability. But the echidna has another amazing adaptation that you can't see. It's a special layer of muscle that wraps around the echidna's whole body.

23   This muscle layer makes the echidna's body very strong. And even more important, it allows the echidna to change its shape. It can roll itself up into a ball. Or it can flatten itself to the thickness of a spiny pancake.

24   That extreme flexibility comes in handy. The echidna can squish itself flat to squeeze into a hiding spot when a predator lurks. It can turn itself into a ball of spines to protect itself from a hungry dingo.

Amazing adaptations!

The echidna's unusual muscles allow it to change shape.

Flat as a pancake!

25   The echidna has one more unique feature. The echidna's body temperature is about 85 to 89 degrees Fahrenheit. (In case you are wondering, your own body temperature is a toasty 98.6 degrees Fahrenheit.) That means the echidna has a lower body temperature than any other mammal.

26   Scientists think that a cool body temperature might help the echidna live longer. Surprisingly, echidnas live as long as 45 years in the wild. Other small mammals don't live nearly as long. When they need to, echidnas can turn down their body temperature even lower than normal. When they do this, all their body functions, such as breathing, heart rate, and digestion, slow down too. This state is called torpor, and it's a bit like hibernation.

27   When in torpor, the echidna uses less energy. So it needs less food. This is useful during the winter, when prey is harder to find. It's also helpful during times of crisis, such as when a forest fire occurs.

28   Scientists think this trait is one reason that the echidna has managed to survive. But it's just one of the adaptations that makes the tiny, spiny echidna one of the most amazing creatures on Earth.

CLOSE READ

Synthesize Information
Underline details from more than one paragraph that you can integrate for better understanding of a topic.

Hollow logs can provide a short-beaked echidna both food and shelter.

Wade Hudson has written more than 25 books for children and young adults. The books often tell about the lives of African Americans and people of color. Wade and his wife have a company that publishes books too. They think good books make a difference in children's lives.

The Very Peculiar Platypus

Preview Vocabulary

As you read *The Very Peculiar Platypus*, look for more uses of the vocabulary words from *The Weird and Wonderful Echidna*, and pay attention to this additional word. Notice how it helps you understand a concept related to the topic.

> **sense**

Read and Compare

Before you read the second **informational text**, establish a purpose for reading. Be sure to follow these strategies as you read this text.

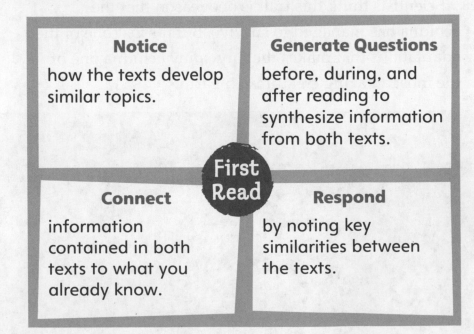

Notice
how the texts develop similar topics.

Generate Questions
before, during, and after reading to synthesize information from both texts.

First Read

Connect
information contained in both texts to what you already know.

Respond
by noting key similarities between the texts.

The Very Peculiar Platypus

by Wade Hudson

AUDIO

ANNOTATE

Synthesize Information

Underline text that you can combine with evidence from *The Weird and Wonderful Echidna* to increase your understanding of a topic.

1   In the late 1700s, British scientists got their first glimpse of a platypus. Or rather, they received a platypus "specimen" that someone had sent from Australia. At first, they thought it was a joke. It looked as if someone had stitched a duck's bill and webbed feet to the skin of an otter or beaver.

2   The platypus does look as if it were put together by a mad scientist. However, its seemingly strange collection of features and adaptations helps the platypus to survive in its Australian home.

A Most Unlikely Mammal

3   The platypus is a mammal, just like a mouse or a dog. It is a warm-blooded animal with a backbone, and it is covered with fur.

4   The average platypus is about 18 inches long, from nose to tail. It weighs anywhere from 1.5 to around 5 pounds. Males are generally larger than females. A platypus may live 13 or more years in the wild and 20 or more in captivity.

A platypus does not have teeth. Instead, it has grinding plates inside its mouth.

5   A platypus spends as much as 10 hours a day in the water. Therefore, lakes, rivers, and streams are always part of a platypus's habitat. A platypus usually forages, or hunts for food, at night. It swims underwater in search of insects, shellfish, and worms. A single dive usually lasts for a minute or two. While underwater, the platypus collects food from the river bottom and stores it in cheek pouches.

6   When not looking for food, the platypus shelters in its burrow. A platypus burrow is usually built in the bank of a river or stream. Sometimes, a platypus uses rocky spots along the edge of the water as shelter. At times, it may make its burrow under logs or among the roots of a tree for protection.

7   In terms of size, traits, and behavior, the platypus is much like other mammals. But this is where the similarities end.

CLOSE READ

Vocabulary in Context

Context clues can help you determine the meanings of multiple-meaning words and words that can be used as different parts of speech.

Underline context clues that help you define *burrow* as it is used in paragraph 6.

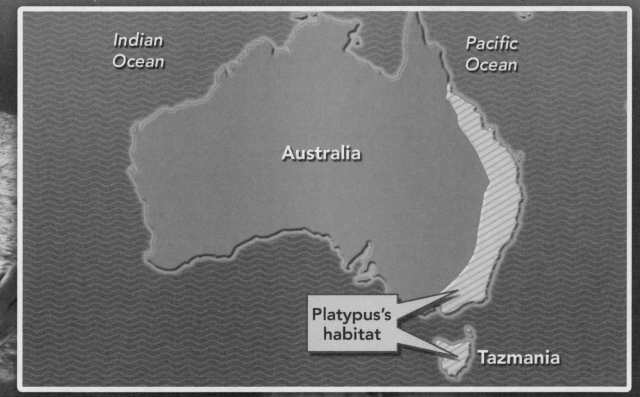

Indian Ocean

Pacific Ocean

Australia

Platypus's habitat

Tazmania

Synthesize Information

<u>Underline</u> information that supports an idea in the previous selection about monotremes.

8   The platypus is a special kind of mammal called a monotreme. The only other monotreme is the echidna, also called the spiny anteater. Like the platypus, the echidna is found in Australia, though echidnas also live in New Guinea. All other mammals give birth to live young. However, monotremes lay eggs. This is just one of many characteristics that make the platypus unusual.

Ducklike Features

9   The platypus's ducklike bill is its most notable feature. And its webbed feet are just as striking. Its bill and feet make it look more like a strange bird than a mammal.

10   However, these features play important roles in survival. Because the platypus hunts for food underwater, swimming skills are vital to survival. A platypus's webbed feet make it an excellent swimmer. Using a rowing motion—first one front foot, then the other—the animal moves easily through the water. It can also hover in one spot, even against the current, while it searches for something to eat.

The platypus's bill is flexible but strong. The animal uses it to push dirt aside when burrowing in riverbanks.

11   Underwater, a platypus closes its eyes, ears, and nostrils. But how can the animal find food? Here is where the platypus's extraordinary bill comes into play. Unlike a duck's hard bill, a platypus's bill is rubbery. It serves as the platypus's sense organ when under the water. The bill has sensors that pick up electrical signals from prey.

Eggs Like a Reptile

12   Platypus eggs aren't like the hard, oval eggs that most birds lay. Instead, platypus eggs are similar to the round, leathery eggs that reptiles such as lizards and turtles lay. The leathery shells are flexible. They are less likely to break during incubation than a hard-shelled egg would be.

13   The female platypus lays one to three eggs. She lays the eggs in a deep burrow and incubates them for about 10 days. When the baby platypuses hatch, they are naked and blind. Only the female platypus cares for the young. Like other mammals, the female platypus feeds milk to her young. When the platypuses are three to four months old, they leave the burrow. At that point, they have a full coat of fur. They have to learn how to swim and find food for themselves.

CLOSE READ

Synthesize Information

Underline information that you can integrate with details from the previous text to better understand how monotremes find food.

sense related to sight, sound, touch, taste, or smell

A platypus egg is about the same diameter as a dime.

Synthesize Information

<u>Underline</u> details you can combine with information from other paragraphs to answer a question about where you can find monotremes.

Platypus Poison

14   The male platypus has a particular feature that the female does not share. Like some species of insects, spiders, and snakes, the male platypus has venom. Sharp spurs on the heels of its hind feet deliver the venom, which is produced by a special gland in the male's thigh. Given a choice, a platypus dives underwater to escape a predator. Or it dashes down a burrow. But if there is no choice, a male platypus uses its spurs to protect itself.

A male platypus also uses its spurs when competing with other males for mates or territory.

A Well-Adapted Oddity

15   The platypus might be the oddest-looking creature on Earth. It seems to be part duck, otter, and beaver. And part snake and spider, too. It's a hodgepodge of strange features that don't seem to belong together.

16   It shares the basic features of all mammals. But, unlike other mammals, the platypus does not give birth to live young. It lays leathery eggs instead. The duckbill and webbed feet make it well suited for its habitat. And, similar to a spider or snake, a platypus can defend itself with venom.

17   The platypus looks like an animal made up of spare parts. But these seemingly unlikely adaptations allow the platypus to find food, protect itself, and reproduce successfully. This ensures the survival of these fascinating creatures.

CLOSE READ

Monitor Comprehension

Highlight a text feature you can use with a fix-up strategy to improve comprehension.

Develop Vocabulary

In scientific informational texts, such as *The Weird and Wonderful Echidna* and *The Very Peculiar Platypus*, authors use domain-specific words, or words related to a particular topic. These words help the reader understand the scientific ideas and concepts in a text.

My TURN Complete the word web. In each circle, define the science vocabulary word and then write a sentence using the word.

unique

Definition:

unusual, one of a kind

Example Sentence:

Echidnas are unique mammals because they lay eggs and have beaks.

adaptations

Definition:

Example Sentence:

Domain: Science

burrow

Definition:

Example Sentence:

sense

Definition:

Example Sentence:

Check for Understanding

My TURN Look back at the text to answer the questions.

1. What features of *The Weird and Wonderful Echidna* and *The Very Peculiar Platypus* tell you that these are informational texts?

2. Explain the author's purpose in each text. How does evidence in each text support each purpose?

3. Cite two pieces of text evidence that show the similarities between the two monotremes.

4. Synthesize what you learned about monotremes from both texts.

Synthesize Information

Readers may think one way about a topic before they begin reading. As they read, they gather information and ideas. During this process, they combine, or **synthesize**, information that may lead them to change their thinking or create new understandings.

1. **My TURN** Go to the Close Read notes in both texts and underline the parts that give important information about each animal.

2. **Text Evidence** Use your notes to show how your thinking has changed.

Before Reading I Thought . . .

The Weird and Wonderful Echidna	*The Very Peculiar Platypus*

Now I Think. . .

Monitor Comprehension

While reading, readers **monitor comprehension** to make sure they understand a text. If a section is confusing or difficult, readers ask themselves questions to clarify their understanding.

To monitor comprehension by asking questions, focus on areas that caused confusion during a first or second read. Ask, *Where did my confusion begin?* Then start rereading a paragraph or two before that section. Note topic sentences and supporting details. When you reach the confusing part, ask: *Does this relate to ideas in another paragraph? How does this section relate to the ones before and after it?*

1. **My TURN** Go back to the Close Read notes and highlight text that causes you to slow down or ask a question.

2. **Text Evidence** Use your highlighted evidence to answer your questions and complete the chart.

What I Know	What I Did not Understand	What I Learned After Rereading

Reflect and Share

Talk About It This week you read about a unique group: the monotremes. What other animals have you read about in other texts? Did they use their adaptations like the echidna and the platypus do? Integrate, or combine, information from several texts to express and support your opinion about the best animal adaptations.

Communicate Ideas During a discussion, you can make your opinion more convincing by expressing your ideas clearly and using formal English. To do this, take notes on your sources and clearly phrase your ideas before you discuss them.

Use these sentence starters to help you form your opinion:

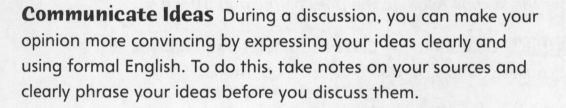

My favorite animal to read about was . . .

The best adaptation was . . .

Next, discuss your opinion with your small group. Did your group members make interesting points that you had not thought of? Consider how the information they provided changed your opinions.

Weekly Question

How do adaptations make animals unique?

Academic Vocabulary

Parts of speech are categories of words. They include **nouns**, **verbs**, **adjectives**, and **adverbs**. Many words can act as more than one part of speech. For example, *classified* can be an adjective or the past tense of the verb *classify*. The verb *organize* can be turned into a noun by changing the ending from *-e* to *-ation*.

My TURN For each sentence,

1. **Underline** the form of one of your academic vocabulary words.

2. **Identify** the word's part of speech.

3. **Write** your own sentence using the same base word but as a different part of speech.

Sentences	Part of Speech
The family <u>survived</u> the storm.	verb
I am taking a wilderness **survival** course.	adjective
Debbie's newest acquisition was a piece of quartz.	
The umbrella defended the twins against the rain.	

Latin Roots *terr, rupt, tract, aqua, dict*

Some words in English have roots from other languages, such as Latin. Knowing the origin of words and word parts can help you define unfamiliar words. For example, the **Latin root** *terr* means "land." If you know the Latin root *terr*, you can define words with this root, such as *territory*, which means "an area of land."

My TURN Read the chart. Add two related words for each root. Then determine and explain the meaning of the related words to a partner. Use a print or online dictionary to check your definitions if needed.

Latin Root	Root Meaning	Related Words
terr	land	territory
rupt	break	disrupt
tract	drag, pull	tractor
aqua	water	aquarium
dict	say	dictation

Read Like a Writer

Authors choose text structures to support their purposes for writing. For **description text structure**, the author introduces a topic and then provides information about it to inform readers. Authors can inform readers in another way with **cause-and-effect text structure.** The author shows how facts, events, or concepts lead to other facts, events, or concepts.

Model ! Reread paragraph 7 of *The Weird and Wonderful Echidna.*

1. Identify Mike Jung uses description text structure to explain how the echidna uses its beak.

2. Question How does the text structure support the author's purpose?

3. Conclude The descriptive text structure supports the author's purpose by organizing information in a way that is easy to understand.

Reread paragraph 21 of *The Weird and Wonderful Echidna.*

My TURN Follow the steps to explain how the text structure supports the author's purpose.

1. Identify Mike Jung uses _____

to explain _____

2. Question How does the text structure support the author's purpose?

3. Conclude This structure supports the author's purpose because it

_____

_____

Write for a Reader

Writers use text structures to present their ideas in a clear and easy way for their readers.

- Description text structure allows writers to inform readers through details, facts, images, and other information.
- Cause-and-effect text structure allows writers to inform readers by showing the connection between facts, events, or concepts and the facts, events, or concepts that cause them.

Choose a text structure that will complement your ideas.

My TURN Think about the text structures the authors used in this week's texts. Now identify how you can choose and use text structures to inform your own readers about a topic.

1. Choose a topic that you know about or a topic that interests you. What text structure would best showcase your topic and your knowledge?

_____

_____

_____

2. Write a passage about your topic using the text structure you chose. Be sure to emphasize the features of the text structure to support your purpose for writing.

_____

_____

_____

_____

_____

_____

_____

Spell Words with Latin Roots

Some words in English come from Latin. Knowing the **Latin roots**
terr, *rupt*, *tract*, *aqua*, and *dict* can help you spell English words
with these roots. For example, if you know how the Latin root *rupt* is
spelled, then it can help you correctly spell words with this root, such
as *abruptly*.

My TURN Read the words. Spell and sort the words by their
Latin roots.

SPELLING WORDS

attract	distract	distraction	erupt
eruption	disrupt	interrupt	territory
territorial	terrain	traction	abstract
aquatic	aquamarine	aquarium	abrupt
diction	dictionary	dictate	verdict

terr

_____

_____

_____

_____

rupt

_____

_____

_____

_____

dict

_____

_____

_____

_____

tract

_____

_____

_____

_____

aqua

_____

_____

_____

_____

Subject-Verb Agreement

A complete sentence must have subject-verb agreement. A singular subject must have a singular verb, and a plural subject must have a plural verb.

If the subject is a **singular noun**, add *-s* or *-es* to the verb to form the present tense.

> The puppy play<u>s</u> with a chew toy.

> The duck splash<u>es</u> in the pond.

If the subject is a **plural noun**, do not add an ending to the verb to form the present tense.

> The puppies **play** with a chew toy.

> The ducks **splash** in the pond.

My TURN Edit this draft to correct the subject-verb agreement in each sentence.

> Monotremes uses their unusual features to survive. Echidnas uses their beaks and tongues to find prey. They sticks out their spikes for protection. Platypus uses similar adaptations. They also senses food with their beaks. To protect themselves, they swims away or uses their poison.

Edit Complete Sentences

A **complete sentence** is one with a **subject** and a **predicate**. The subject of a sentence is a noun or a pronoun, and the predicate of a sentence is a verb. A complete sentence must have **subject-verb agreement**. A singular subject must have a singular verb, and a plural subject must have a plural verb.

Subject	Verb Rules	Examples
Singular	• Add -s or -es to the present-tense verb to make a singular verb. • Use *is* or *was*.	Rob runs faster than Jewel runs. The big **cat watches** the people passing by. The pilot **is** from Utah. Our bus **driver** was singing a song.
Plural	• Do not add an ending to the present-tense verb. • Use *are* or *were*.	**Ostriches run** beside the jeep. **Bobcats watch** cottontail rabbits. The **pilots are** all women. The racecar **drivers** were taking a break.

My TURN Edit these sentences so that they have subject-verb agreement. Cross out three incorrect words and write the correct words above them.

> The chickens is eating corn. Bailey throw more on the ground, and the
>
> birds runs after the new pieces.

My TURN Apply this skill when you edit the draft of a travel article in your writing notebook.

Edit for Nouns

A **singular noun** names *one* person, place, or thing. A **plural noun** names *more than one* person, place, or thing.

A **common noun**, such as *city*, names any person, place, or thing. Common nouns begin with lowercase letters unless they are at the beginning of a sentence.

A **proper noun**, such as *Chicago*, names a particular person, place, or thing. Proper nouns begin with capital letters. When a proper noun has more than one word, then the first letter of each important word is capitalized (for example, *Statue of Liberty*).

My TURN Edit the nouns in the paragraph to correct capitalization errors and to make nouns singular or plural so they go with the rest of the sentence.

> The world's largest bat colonies is in bracken cave. The Caves is near san antonio, texas. People love to watch the millions of bat fly out at Sunset.

My TURN Correctly capitalize proper nouns when you edit the draft of a travel article in your writing notebook.

Make sure all proper nouns are capitalized in your travel article.

Publish and Celebrate

Writers publish their work for the appropriate audience when they are finished. A travel article may be published in a newspaper, magazine, or online.

My TURN Complete these sentences about your writing experience. Write legibly, or clearly, in cursive so that others can easily read what you write.

My favorite part of writing a travel article was

_____

_____

_____

It is clear from the article that I thought about my audience because

_____

_____

_____

The words and phrases I added to strengthen my article include

_____

_____

_____

The best multimedia to go with my article would be

_____

_____

_____

Prepare for Assessment

My TURN Follow a plan as you prepare to write a travel article in response to a prompt. Use your own paper.

1. **Study the prompt.**

   You will receive an assignment called a writing prompt. Carefully read the prompt below. Highlight the type of writing you must do. <u>Underline</u> the topic you must write about.

   Prompt: Write a feature article about a nearby travel destination where visitors can learn about local plants or animals.

2. **Brainstorm.**

   List three destinations you could write about. Then highlight your favorite.

3. **Assemble details and photographs.**

4. **Map out your article.**

   Lead Paragraph → Next Paragraph → Next Paragraph → Conclusion

5. **Write your draft.**

   Write a first-draft headline and article. Remember to incorporate photographs, captions, and multimedia if appropriate.

6. **Revise and edit your article.**

   Apply the skills and rules you have learned to polish your writing.

Always keep your audience in mind when you write a travel article.

Assessment

My TURN Before you write a travel article for your assessment, rate how well you understand the skills you have learned in this unit. Go back and review any skills you mark "No."

		Yes!	No
Ideas and Organization	◎ I can brainstorm and plan an article.	☐	☐
	◎ I can write a lead paragraph.	☐	☐
	◎ I can organize relevant details into paragraphs and sections.	☐	☐
	◎ I can choose illustrations and photos.	☐	☐
Craft	◎ I can convey a clear idea about a destination.	☐	☐
	◎ I can include different types of details.	☐	☐
	◎ I can write a headline.	☐	☐
	◎ I can use precise language and vocabulary.	☐	☐
	◎ I can use transition words.	☐	☐
	◎ I can use linking words and phrases.	☐	☐
	◎ I can incorporate multimedia.	☐	☐
Conventions	◎ I can capitalize and use nouns correctly.	☐	☐
	◎ I can edit for subject-verb agreement.	☐	☐
	◎ I can use adverbs effectively.	☐	☐
	◎ I can use coordinating conjunctions correctly.	☐	☐

UNIT THEME
Adaptations

TURNand**TALK** **QUESTION THE ANSWERS** Read the sentence that relates to each selection. Then, with a partner, review the selection and write a question that could be answered by the sentence. Finally, talk to your partner about how the questions and answers relate to the theme, *Adaptations*.

WEEK 3

from **Minn of the Mississippi**

She is the "monster" in the boys' swimming hole.

_____

⭐ **BOOK CLUB**

WEEK 2

Animal Mimics

This kind of animal copies the appearance, action, or sound of another animal.

_____

⭐ **BOOK CLUB**

WEEK 1

Feathers: Not Just for Flying

These feathers attract attention and maybe even a mate.

_____

BOOK CLUB

from **Butterfly Eyes and Other Secrets of the Meadow**

Monarch butterflies lay their eggs on this plant that has pods and lavender flowers.

WEEK 4

BOOK CLUB

WEEK 5

The Weird and Wonderful Echidna and The Very Peculiar Platypus

This country is home to both the echidna and the platypus.

Essential Question

MyTURN

In your notebook, answer the Essential Question: How do living things adapt to the world around them?

BOOK CLUB

WEEK 6 *Project*

Now it is time to apply what you learned about Adaptations in your WEEK 6 PROJECT: Saving Species!

Saving SPECIES

Activity

Create a poster about an endangered animal. Research important information about the animal, such as what it eats, where it lives, what adaptations it has made to survive, and why it is now endangered.

Research Articles

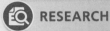

With your partner, read "Adapting to Urban Habitats" to generate and clarify questions you have about the inquiry topic. Next, begin developing a research plan to help you create your poster. Be sure to share responsibilities with your partner.

1 **Adapting to Urban Habitats**

2 **An Unlikely Friendship**

3 **Biomimicry: Shaping the Shinkansen**

Generate Questions

COLLABORATE Read "Adapting to Urban Habitats" and generate three questions you have about the article. With your partner, answer any questions you can before sharing them with the class.

1. _____

2. _____

3. _____

Use Academic Words

Work with your partner to complete the chart. If appropriate, use this vocabulary when you create your poster.

Academic Vocabulary	Word Forms	Word in Context
survive	survives survival survived	Plants need water and sunlight for their **survival**.
defense	defenses defend defender	The **defender** blocked the rebound shot.
classified	classify classifies classification	Ladybugs can be **classified** by the number of spots they have.
acquire	acquires acquired acquisition	Animals **acquire**, or learn, survival skills from other animals.
sufficient	sufficiently insufficient self-sufficient	The family gathered **sufficient** supplies for their camping trip.

Just the Facts

Informational texts should include lots of facts.

People write **informational texts** to give a reader facts. When reading informational texts, you can gather information by identifying or using

- a main idea
- supporting details or evidence, such as facts and examples
- text features, such as headings and pictures
- a logical text structure, such as description, compare and contrast, or cause and effect

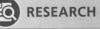 RESEARCH

COLLABORATE Read "An Unlikely Friendship" with your partner. Then answer the questions about the article and the information the author uses.

1. Who is the intended audience for the article?

_____

_____

2. What does the author want the reader to think?

_____

_____

3. Which text structure does the author use? How does this help you understand the text?

_____

_____

_____

Plan Your Research

COLLABORATE Before you begin researching your animal, you will need to come up with a research plan. Use this activity to plan how you will look for information for your poster.

Definition	Examples
TEXT STRUCTURE shows how ideas are related. • Use **compare-and-contrast text structure** to show similarities and differences. • Use **description text structure** to give images and details. Read the two examples in the right column. Then, with your partner, identify the best way to structure information on your poster.	• Both butterflies use mimicry, but they use it in different ways. Compare-and-contrast text structure • Viceroy butterfly caterpillars store acid in their bodies. This acid gives the butterflies a bitter taste, which keeps birds away. Description text structure Which text structure would work best to organize your ideas?
EVIDENCE Develop and support your ideas with • facts • examples • quotations • pictures	**Fact:** A volcano is a landform with an opening. **Example:** Japan, Indonesia, and Hawaii are all places that have volcanoes. **Quote:** "Four volcanoes could erupt this year," wrote noted volcanologist Elena Marquez. **Pictures:** photograph of a volcano, map showing active volcanoes

With your partner, list some possible options for finding information for your poster.

BIG DATA

You can use a **library database** to find the information you need. You may get a lot of pages that are *not* useful to you. When that happens, use the advanced search buttons. Using advanced search is a lot like giving specific directions.

> **EXAMPLE** DeShawn is giving Lindy instructions to help her find a certain book in the bookcase.
> **DeShawn:** "Stand facing the bookcase. Now, look to your left. Next, look up one shelf. Take out the tallest book. It should have a volcano on the cover."

Notice that DeShawn makes the instructions more specific as Lindy gets closer. Similarly, when you use advanced search buttons, you are giving the database specific directions about what information to find.

In an advanced search, you can identify key words, words not to include, language, audience, date published, format, and availability. By filling out an advanced search form, you are more likely to get results that are relevant to your topic.

Advanced Search   Search Clear

Enter search terms in at least one of the fields below

Keyword _____

but do not include:

Keyword _____

Narrow your search (optional)

Year [ ] to [ ]
e.g. 1971 e.g. 1977

Audience [ ] Any audience [ ] Juvenile [ ] Adult

Content [ ] Any content [ ] Fiction [ ] Non-fiction [ ] Textbooks

COLLABORATE Give your partner instructions to get from one side of your classroom to the other. Give the directions one at a time. Have your partner carry out each instruction before you give the next one. Restate any instructions as needed. Then change roles so your partner is directing you. When you are finished, discuss which directions were easiest to follow. Tell your partner how this activity is like using a library database to narrow down a search.

Now apply the concept to your research. In the advanced search fields, write key words and anything else that will help you narrow down your research. Put these skills into practice the next time you use a library database.

Advanced Search

Search   Clear

Enter search terms in at least one of the fields below

[Keyword] _____

but do not include:

[Keyword] _____

Narrow your search (optional)

Year [   ] to [   ]

Audience [ ] Any audience   [ ] Juvenile   [ ] Adult

Content [ ] Any content   [ ] Fiction   [ ] Non-fiction   [ ] Textbooks

Get NOTICED!

One type of informational text is an **informational poster**. With a poster, writers can display information in a way that will attract the audience's attention. When you create an informational poster, you will

- Include a title related to your topic
- Use bright colors and big letters
- Use images such as photographs, drawings, diagrams, and graphs
- Express information using sentences and short paragraphs

COLLABORATE Study the Student Model. Talk with your partner about how you can make a poster that helps readers learn more about your topic.

Now You Try It!

Discuss the checklist with your partner. Work together to follow the steps as you create your poster.

Make sure your informational poster

☐ includes facts about your animal that are paraphrased, or put in your own words, from your research

☐ includes information about your animal's diet, habitat, and adaptations

☐ includes both text and graphic features

☐ is logically organized

☐ is engaging and easy to read

Student Model

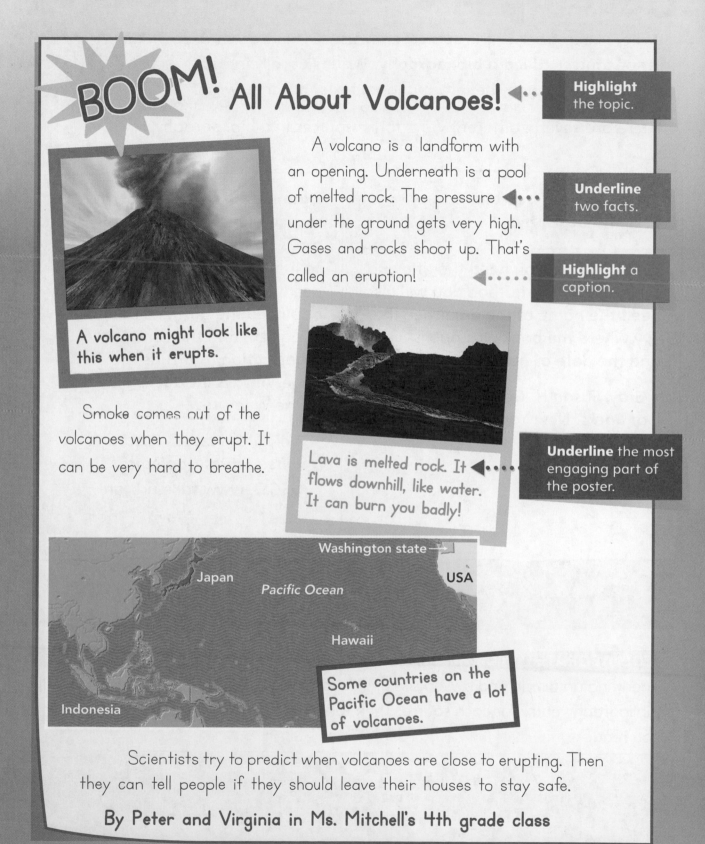

BOOM! All About Volcanoes!

A volcano is a landform with an opening. Underneath is a pool of melted rock. The pressure under the ground gets very high. Gases and rocks shoot up. That's called an eruption!

Highlight the topic.

Underline two facts.

Highlight a caption.

A volcano might look like this when it erupts.

Smoke comes out of the volcanoes when they erupt. It can be very hard to breathe.

Lava is melted rock. It flows downhill, like water. It can burn you badly!

Underline the most engaging part of the poster.

Washington state →

Japan

Pacific Ocean

USA

Hawaii

Some countries on the Pacific Ocean have a lot of volcanoes.

Indonesia

Scientists try to predict when volcanoes are close to erupting. Then they can tell people if they should leave their houses to stay safe.

By Peter and Virginia in Ms. Mitchell's 4th grade class

Develop a Bibliography

Writers keep track of the sources they use. Often they make a list of sources called a **bibliography**. Writers usually include a bibliography with the informational texts that they write.

There are several different ways to list sources in a bibliography.

Example for a book listed in a bibliography:	Example for an Internet source in a bibliography:
To list a book, you need the title and the name of the author. You will also need the name of the publisher, the city where the book was published, and the date of publication. • Gray, Susan H. *Geology: The Study of Rocks*. New York, NY: Scholastic, 2012.	To list an Internet source, you need the name of the article. You also need the author's name, if it is given, and the company or organization that runs the Web page. Always include the address of the Web site. • "Volcano Hazards Program." *United States Geological Survey (USGS)*, www.fake.url.com

COLLABORATE With your partner, read "Biomimicry: Shaping the Shinkansen." Then find an article and a Web site on the same topic. Develop and record a bibliography entry for each source. Then take notes on any interesting information you read.

COLLABORATE Read the information about volcanoes, including the bibliography entry. Then answer the questions.

Around the world there are many very old volcanoes that no longer erupt. Some of these volcanoes are dead and will not erupt again. These are called extinct. Others can be inactive for as long as 50,000 years and then reawaken. These are called dormant.

Source: Simon, Seymour. *Volcanoes*. New York, NY: Children's Books, 1998.

1. What is the title of the book given in the bibliography entry?

_____

_____

2. In what city was that book published?

_____

_____

3. What steps could you take to evaluate this source?

_____

_____

Incorporate MEDIA

Informational posters need visuals to support the information they present. Adding maps, diagrams, and pictures can make your poster much more appealing to your audience.

Include **photographs** of your animal so your audience knows what the animal looks like. Photos will also give information such as the shape of the animal's mouth and the number of legs it has.

Maps can be very helpful for showing where your animal lives. Shade the places where the animal makes its home.

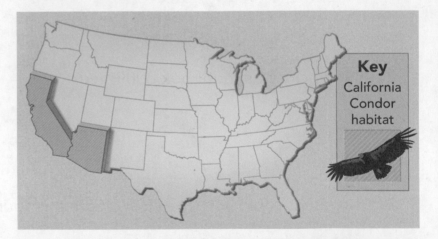

Key
California Condor habitat

You can also include a **diagram**. A diagram might show the den or the nest where the animal lives. A diagram could also show the foods that your animal eats.

COLLABORATE Work with your partner to decide what types of visuals would work best for your poster. Remember that you need to provide information about your animal's habitat, diet, and adaptations, along with interesting facts about your animal.

In the graphic organizer below, write what you want to show in different visuals.

Drawing or Photograph	Map	Diagram
Visuals:	Visuals:	Visuals:

Other Visuals:

Revise

Revise for Clarity Reread your poster with your partner. Have you

- [ ] included facts about your topic?
- [ ] given interesting information about your topic?
- [ ] presented your information using a clear text structure?
- [ ] made a poster that appeals to the reader's eye?
- [ ] included a list of your sources?

Revise Language

The students who created the **Student Model** informational poster reread an earlier draft of their work. They saw that they needed to make some changes so their writing would be clearer and easier to read.

A volcano might look like this when it erupt. ^s

When t ,g
~~The~~ pressure under the ground gets very high. ~~Gases~~ and rock shoot ~~up. They come~~ out the opening.

they erupt.
Smoke comes out of the volcanoes when ~~it erupts.~~

Edit

Conventions Read your text again. Did you use language conventions correctly?

☐ compound sentences

☐ complex sentences

☐ common and proper nouns

☐ singular and plural nouns

☐ subject-verb agreement

Peer Review

COLLABORATE Exchange posters with another pair. Read the other pair's poster, and look at the visuals. Look for all the required information, and check that the information is clear. Listen as they practice presenting the poster. Show that you understood by paraphrasing what they said. Provide feedback about how they can improve their presentation.

Time to Celebrate!

COLLABORATE Present your poster to another group. Make eye contact with your audience as you present. Speak clearly, and use a natural speaking rate and normal volume. Indicate the visuals and read any captions you wrote.

Allow time for students in the other group to make comments and ask questions. How did they react? What did they like about your presentation? What suggestions for changes or improvements did they make? Write their reactions here.

_____

_____

_____

_____

Reflect on Your Project

My TURN Think about your poster. What parts of the poster do you think are most effective? Which parts could be improved? How might you improve them? Write your ideas here.

Strengths _____

_____

Areas of Improvement _____

_____

Reflect on Your Goals

Look back at your unit goals.
Use a different color to rate yourself again.

Reflect on Your Reading

Of the adaptations described in this unit, which one would you most like to learn more about? Explain.

_____

_____

_____

_____

_____

Reflect on Your Writing

During this unit, what new ideas or strategies did you learn that helped you improve your writing? Explain.

_____

_____

_____

_____

_____

How to Use a Glossary

This glossary can help you understand the meaning, part of speech, pronunciation, and syllabication of some of the words in this book. The entries in this glossary are in alphabetical order. The guide words at the top of each page show the first and last words on the page. If you cannot find a word, check a print or digital dictionary. You would use a dictionary just as you would a glossary. To use a digital resource, type the word you are looking for in the search box at the top of the page.

Example glossary entry:

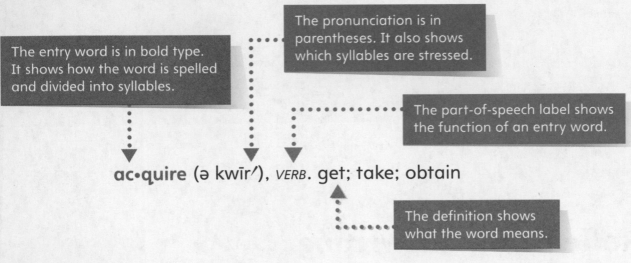

The entry word is in bold type. It shows how the word is spelled and divided into syllables.

The pronunciation is in parentheses. It also shows which syllables are stressed.

The part-of-speech label shows the function of an entry word.

ac•quire (ə kwīr′), VERB. get; take; obtain

The definition shows what the word means.

My TURN Find and write the meaning of the word *survive*.

Write the syllabication of the word. _____
Use the pronunciation guide to help you say the word aloud.
What other words do you know that share the same base word as *survive*?

TURN and TALK With a partner, discuss how you can use a print or digital dictionary to find the meaning of a word that is not in this glossary.

Aa

ac•quire (ə kwīr′), *VERB*. get; take; obtain

ad•ap•ta•tions (ad′ap tā′shənz), *NOUN*. changes that make a plant or animal better suited to an environment

ar•ranged (ə rānjd′), *VERB*. organized or designed

as•sem•bled (ə sem′bəld), *VERB*. put or brought together

Bb

bris•tle (briss′əl), *ADJECTIVE*. short and rough

brit•tle (brit′l), *ADJECTIVE*. very easily broken

bur•row (bėr′ō), *VERB*. dig a hole

Cc

ca•pac•i•ty (kə pas′ə tē), *NOUN*. the ability to contain something

Pronunciation Guide

Use the pronunciation guide to help you pronounce the words correctly.

a in *hat*	ō in *open*	sh in *she*
ā in *age*	ȯ in *all*	th in *thin*
â in *care*	ô in *order*	ŦH in *then*
ä in *far*	oi in *oil*	zh in *measure*
e in *let*	ou in *out*	ə = a in *about*
ē in *equal*	u in *cup*	ə = e in *taken*
ėr in *term*	u̇ in *put*	ə = i in *pencil*
i in *it*	ü in *rule*	ə = o in *lemon*
ī in *ice*	ch in *child*	ə = u in *circus*
o in *hot*	ng in *long*	

chromosomes • DNA

chro•mo•somes (krō′mə sōmz), *NOUN*. parts of DNA in cells that hold the genes

clas•si•fied (klas′ə fīd), *VERB*. categorized; grouped with

com•par•i•son (kəm par′ə sən), *NOUN*. examination of things to see how they are similar

con•fi•dence (kon′fə dəns), *NOUN*. a feeling that a person can succeed or do well

con•tour (kon′tu̇r), *ADJECTIVE*. related to the shape or outline of something

con•trib•ute (kən trib′yüt), *VERB*. donate; assist

Dd

de•fense (di fens′), *NOUN*. someone or something that protects

de•scent (di sent′), *NOUN*. the family background or national origin of a person

de•sert•ed (di zėr′tid), *VERB*. left someone or something alone

de•sire (di zīr′), *NOUN*. a powerful wish or longing for something

des•o•late (des′ə lit), *ADJECTIVE*. empty, lonely, and unhappy

de•ter•mi•na•tion (di tėr′mə nā′shən), *NOUN*. the will to achieve a difficult task

di•vert•ed (də vėr′tid), *VERB*. changed the direction of

DNA *NOUN*. the substance in cells that determines the characteristics of a living thing

drive (drīv), *NOUN.* the ambition or motivation to carry on

du•pli•cate (dü′plə kit), *ADJECTIVE.* exactly the same as another

Ee

en•dur•ance (en dùr′əns), *NOUN.* the ability to keep going

en•vi•ron•ment (en vī′rən mənt), *NOUN.* all the living things and conditions of a place

ex•cel (ek sel′), *VERB.* do well or be the best at something

ex•cret•ed (ek skrē′tid), *VERB.* separated and removed from the body

ex•posed (ek spōzd′), *ADJECTIVE.* revealed; unprotected

Hh

hab•it (hab′it), *NOUN.* usual practice

hab•i•tat (hab′ə tat), *NOUN.* the place where a living thing lives or grows

Ii

i•den•ti•cal (ī den′tə kəl), *ADJECTIVE.* appearing to be exactly the same

in•de•pend•ence (in′di pən′dəns), *NOUN.* freedom from being controlled or needing help from others

in•tern•ment (in tėrn′mənt), *ADJECTIVE.* related to confinement, as if in a prison, often during a war

Mm

mim•ic•ry (mim′ik rē), *NOUN.* the ability to look or act like something else

mon•o•tremes (mon′ə trēmz), *NOUN.* animals that are mammals but lay eggs

mo•ti•va•tion (mō′tə vā′shən), *NOUN.* a reason for doing something

Pp

pov•er•ty (pov′ər tē), *NOUN*. the state of being extremely poor

prey (prā), *NOUN*. an animal hunted by others for food

pur•sued (pər süd′), *VERB*. worked without stopping to get or accomplish something

Rr

ra•di•a•tion (rā′dē ā′shən), *NOUN*. energy that travels in the form of waves outward from a source, such as the sun

rap•ids (rap′idz), *NOUN*. very fast-moving parts of a river

re•mark•a•ble (ri mär′kə bəl), *ADJECTIVE*. extraordinary or outstanding

Ss

sense (sens), *ADJECTIVE*. related to sight, sound, touch, taste, or smell

se•vere (sə vir′), *ADJECTIVE*. harsh; serious

shal•low (shal′ō), *ADJECTIVE*. not very deep

shim•mer•ing (shim′ər ing), *ADJECTIVE*. shining with a soft, flickering light

sig•nif•i•cant (sig nif′ə kənt), *ADJECTIVE*. important; relevant

spe•cial•ized (spesh′ə līzd), *VERB*. gained specific knowledge

spe•cies (spē′shēz), *NOUN*. categories of living things

spec•ta•tors (spec′tā tərz), *NOUN*. people who watch an event

steeped (stēpd), *VERB*. soaked; drenched

strug•gled (strug'əld), *VERB*. made a great and difficult effort

suf•fi•cient (sə fish'ent), *ADJECTIVE*. enough for a particular purpose

sur•vive (sər vīv'), *VERB*. stay alive; live through a dangerous event

sys•tem (sis'təm), *NOUN*. set of connected things

Tt

ten•der (ten'dər), *ADJECTIVE*. soft or gentle; easily damaged

treach•er•ous (trech'ər əs), *ADJECTIVE*. unsafe because of hidden dangers

Uu

ul•tra•vi•o•let (ul'trə vī'ə lit), *ADJECTIVE*. related to a color that is invisible to the human eye

u•nique (yü nēk'), *ADJECTIVE*. unusual; unlike anything else

Vv

ves•sels (ves'əlz), *NOUN*. tubes or passageways carrying fluid around an organism; containers

Text

Abrams Books
Barbed Wire Baseball written by Marissa Moss and Illustrated by Yuko Shimizu. Text copyright (c) 2013 Marissa Moss. Illustrations copyright (c) 2013 Yuko Shimizu. Used with the permission of Express Permissions on behalf of Abrams Books, an imprint of Harry N. Abrams, Inc., New York. All rights reserved.

Don Brown
Rare Treasure: Mary Anning and Her Remarkable Discoveries by Don Brown. Published by Houghton Mifflin. Used with permission from the author.

Charlesbridge Publishing
Feathers: Not Just for Flying, text copyright© 2014 by Melissa Stewart. Illustration copyright© 2014 by Sarah S. Brannen. Used with permission by Charlesbridge Publishing, Inc. 85 Main Street Watertown, MA 02472 All rights reserved.

Cricket Media
Twins in Space by Rebecca Boyle. Used with permission from Cricket Media.

HarperCollins Publishers
Reaching for the Moon, text copyright (c) 2005 by Buzz Aldrin. Used by permission of HarperCollins Publishers.

Houghton Mifflin Harcourt Publishing Company
Minn of the Mississippi by Holling C. Holling. Copyright© 1951 by Holling C. Holling, renewed 1979 by Lucille Webster Holling. Reprinted by permission of Houghton Mifflin Harcourt Publishing Company. All rights reserved. Bubble Song, Sap Song, Heavenly, Ultraviolet, Milkweed and Butterflies, The Gray Ones, We Are Waiting, and Deer and Trees from Butterfly Eyes and Other Secrets of the Meadow by Joyce Sidman, illustrated by Beth Krommes. Text copyright© 2006 by Joyce Sidman. Illustrations copyright© 2006 by Beth Krommes. Reprinted by permission of Houghton Mifflin Harcourt Publishing Company. All rights reserved.

The Rosen Publishing Group Inc.
Animal Mimics by Marie Racanelli, 2010. Reprinted by permission from Rosen Publishing Group.

Photographs

Photo locators denoted as follows Top (T), Center (C), Bottom (B), Left (L), Right (R), Background (Bkgd)

8 (Bkgd) Grigorii Pisotsckii/Shutterstock, (BL) Hurst Photo/ Shutterstock; 9 Stocktrek Images/Getty Images; 14 (TR) Peiyang/Shutterstock, (BL) LouieLea/Shutterstock, (BR) Bernhard Richter/Shutterstock; 15 (TL) Anderm/ Shutterstock, (BR) Fer Gregory/Shutterstock; 18 (TL) NASA/Kim Shiflett; 50 (Bkgd) Rawpixel.com/Shutterstock, (TL) Dervin Witmer/Shutterstock, (TR) Alfred Bartnik/ Shutterstock, (BL) Babaroga/Shutterstock, (BR) Max Topchii/Shutterstock; 51 (T) Lakov Filimonov/Shutterstock, (B) Wavebreakmedia/Shutterstock; 84 (Bkgd) Nienora/ Shutterstock, (C) JSC/NASA, (TL) Surachai/Shutterstock, (B) WhiteJack/Shutterstock; 85 (T) Leonid Dorfman/123RF, (B) Cathy Yeulet /123RF; 90 (L) NASA, (R) Maridav/Shutterstock; 90-99 Vladi333/Shutterstock; 96 (B) Science Picture Co/ Superstock; 116 (Bkgd) JBoy/Shutterstock, Gurunars/ Shutterstock, (T) Sergey Uryadnikov/Shutterstock, (C) Peachananr/Shutterstock, (B) Aureliy/Shutterstock; 117 (T) Dossyl/Shutterstock, (C) Nathapol Kongseang/Shutterstock, (B) Twinlynx/Shutterstock; 121 Sam DCruz/Shutterstock; 122 Nigel Pavitt/John Warburton-Lee Photography/Alamy Stock Photo; 124 Simon Maina/AFP/Getty Images; 125 Antony Njuguna/Reuters/Alamy Stock Photo; 126 Roger Sedres/Alamy Stock Photo; 130 Michael Steele/Contour/ Getty Images; 132 Polifoto/Alamy Stock Photo; 133 Frank Rocco/Alamy Stock Photo; 135 Jessica Rinaldi/The Boston Globe/Getty Images; 152 (T) Oleksandr Kovalchuk/123RF, (C) DRogatnev/Shutterstock, (B) Topic Images Inc./Getty Images; 152 (Bkgd) Jess Kraft/Shutterstock; 153 (B) Wisanu Boonrawd/Shutterstock; 156 Used with permission from Express Permissions; 200 America/Alamy Stock Photo; 204 (L) Ezra_Lathouwers/Shutterstock, (C) Wdnet/iStock/ Getty Images, (R) Oknarit/iStock/Getty Images; 207 (BR) Monkey Business Images/Shutterstock; 213 Ulrike Schmitt-Hartmann/The Image Bank/Getty Images; 216 Doug Lemke/Shutterstock; 216 Puhhha/Shutterstock; 217 (Bkgd) Borja Andreu/Shutterstock; 222 (TL) TJ Brown/ Shutterstock, (TR) Snowleopard1/E+/Getty Images, (BL) Moosehenderson/Shutterstock, (BR) Andrea Izzotti/123RF; 222 Chin797/Shutterstock; 223 Don Fink/123RF; 226 Used with permission from Charlesbridge Publishing; 262 Luke Suen/Shutterstock; 262 (L) Sascha Janson/Shutterstock, (R) Supermaw/Shutterstock; 263 (T) Jiri Prochazka/ Shutterstock, (B) Anne Powell/Shutterstock; 267 Avalon/ Photoshot License/Alamy Stock Photo; 269 Darlyne A. Murawski/National Geographic Creative/Alamy Stock Photo; 271 Nechaevkon/Shutterstock; 273 (T) Rusty Dodson/Shutterstock, (B) John Cancalosi/Photolibrary/Getty Images; 275 Leena Robinson/Alamy Stock Photo; 277 Chris Alcock/Shutterstock; 278 Sergey Dubrov/Shutterstock; 281 Hugh Clark/Alamy Stock Photo; 283 Meyers/Blickwinkel/ Alamy Stock Photo; 286 Kamnuan/Shutterstock; 287 Lovely Bird/Shutterstock; 302 (C) Donna Heatfield/Shutterstock; 302 (L) 123RF, (R) Mark Caunt/Shutterstock; 304 (Bkgd) Sap Ibrahim/Shutterstock, (T) Simon Eeman/Shutterstock, (C) Volodymyr Nikitenko/Shutterstock, (B) Topic Images Inc./Getty Images; 336 (Bkgd) Sittipan Suwannabandit/ Shutterstock, (C) PBNJ Productions/Blend Images/Getty Images; 340 Courtesy of Houghton Mifflin Harcourt; 370 (Bkgd) Milan M/Shutterstock, (B) Soaring4031/Shutterstock; 371 (T) Ali Iyoob Photography/Shutterstock, (B) Magnetix/ Shutterstock; 375 Clearviewstock/Shutterstock; 376 Paul Looyen/Shutterstock; 377 Jean-Paul Ferrero/Auscape International Pty Ltd/Alamy Stock Photo; 378 Simon McGill/ Moment Open/Getty Images; 379 Eric Isselee/Shutterstock; 380 Australia, Australian, Australasian, Wildlife, Animal/ Mary Evans Picture Library Ltd/AGE Fotostock; 382 (L) Marc Anderson/Alamy Stock Photo, (R) Steve Lovegrove/ Shutterstock; 383 Tier Und Naturfotografie J und C Sohns/ Photographer's Choice RF/Getty Images; 385 Dave Watts/ Alamy Stock Photo; 387 (T) Marie Read/Science Source; 388 (L) Gerard Lacz/VWPics/Newscom; 389 DEA PICTURE LIBRARY Universal Images Group; 410 Robert Scholl/ Alamy Stock Photo; 414 Mike Kemp/Getty Images; 417 (L) Corey Ford/Stocktrek Images, Inc./Alamy Stock Photo, (R) Beboy/Shutterstock; 418 Suronin/Shutterstock; 420 (L) Marosbauer/123RF, (R) Michael Steden/Shutterstock; 423 Ian Shaw/Alamy Stock Photo.

Illustrations

17, 265 Valentina Belloni; 53, 339 Ilana Exelby; 87, 119, 225, 373 Olga & Aleksey Ivanov; 124 Joe Lemmier; 129 Peter Hoey; 155 Valeria Cis; 207, 210 Karen Minot; 307 Ken Bowser; 370-371 Jun Park; 377, 387, 414-15, 417, 420 Rob Schuster